Intelligent Machinery: Theory and Practice

Intelligent Machinery

THEORY AND PRACTICE

Edited by

IAN BENSON

SRI International

Illustrated by Benny Kandler

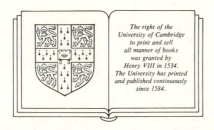

The right of the
University of Cambridge
to print and sell
all manner of books
was granted by
Henry VIII in 1534.
The University has printed
and published continuously
since 1584.

CAMBRIDGE UNIVERSITY PRESS

Cambridge

London   New York   New Rochelle

Melbourne   Sydney

Published by the Press Syndicate of the University of Cambridge
The Pitt Building, Trumpington Street, Cambridge CB2 1RP
32 East 57th Street, New York, NY 10022, USA
10 Stamford Road, Oakleigh, Melbourne 3166, Australia

First published 1986

Printed in Great Britain at the University Press, Cambridge

British Library cataloguing in publication data
Intelligent machinery: theory and practice.
1. Artificial intelligence
1. Benson, Ian
001.53′5   Q335

Library of Congress cataloging in publication data
Main entry under title:
Intelligent machinery.
Papers presented at a conference organized by SRI
International and held in Cambridge, September 1984.
Includes index.
1. Electronic digital computers – Congresses.
2. Artificial intelligence – Congresses. I. Benson,
Ian. II. SRI International.
QA76.5.14886   1985   004   85–12838

ISBN 0 521 30836 4

CONTENTS

CONTRIBUTORS

Ian Benson
Information, Services and
Systems Division
SRI International
NLA Tower,
Addiscombe Road,
Croydon, CRO OXT, UK

Richard Ennals
Fifth Generation Research
Group
Department of Computing
Imperial College, London, UK

Dr. Thomas Garvey
Artificial Intelligence Centre
Computer Science and
Technology Division
SRI International
Menlo Park, CA 94025, USA

Michael Melliar-Smith
Computer Science Laboratory
Computer Science and
Technology Division
SRI International
Menlo Park, CA 94025, USA

Dr. Robert C. Moore
Artificial Intelligence Centre
Computer Science and
Technology Division
SRI International
Menlo Park, CA 94025, USA

Dr. Stanley J. Rosenschein
Artificial Intelligence Centre
Computer Science and
Technology Division
SRI International
Menlo Park, CA 94025, USA

Professor Erik Sandewall
Software Systems Research
Centre
Linköping University
S-58183 Linköping, Sweden

FOREWORD

Information technology's penetration of industry, commerce and society has accelerated with the invention of computers, semiconductors, microelectronic chips. The rate of penetration will continue to accelerate well into the next century as the cost of computer memory falls alongside the reduction in processing costs, as the speed of computing increases, as the communications infrastructure develops to liberate these technologies. We have only just begun to see the impact of these technologies in the factory, the office and the home.

If the proliferation of hardware embodying information technologies is going to be impressive, then the prospective advances in software seem incredible. Advanced computer science – particularly artificial intelligence – will create capabilities to integrate and optimise design, engineering, inventory, assembly, machining, distribution, analysis, planning and management. The factory, office and home of the future are all going to be radically changed by computer integrated manufacture (CIM), office automation and telecommunications. The quality of the software will determine the effectiveness of the hardware systems and the services. Ultimately, this will affect the competitive capabilities of the organisations that sell and use them and the economies to which they belong.

Software – particularly for artificial intelligence purposes – will become a major strategic resource. The indications are that it will not be traded freely across frontiers, which will widen the technology gap opening between Europe on the one hand and Japan and the USA on the other.

This book is a product of a conference, organised by SRI International and held in Cambridge, in the UK in September 1984. The purpose was to identify opportunities for scientific collaboration by reviewing the research agenda of the major national Fifth Generation Research Programmes, focusing on technical questions but touching on the novel institutional arrangements in which the programmes were being carried out.

The three days of discussions were introduced by Brian Oakley, Director of the UK Alvey Programme, Professor Hideo Aiso of the Japanese Fifth Generation Project, and Horst Hünke of the EEC ESPRIT Programme. It was noted that all government and industry initiatives shared several common disabilities; shortage of money and computing equipment, duplication of effort, overlaps and gaps in coverage, training deficiencies and, most of all, a lack of appropriate people. An agenda for collaboration was proposed which built on the work areas described in the book. What was required was a real international dimension in the various national strategies, to enable an accelerated programme of scientific exchanges, workshops and joint projects.

We are grateful for the assistance of all those who took part in leading discussions at the conference. In particular, Sir Hermann Bondi, Master, Churchill College, Professor Roger Needham & Karen Sparck Jones, Cambridge University, UK, Geoffrey Robinson, IBM Science Centre, UK, Horst Hünke, ESPRIT Programme, EEC, Brian Oakley, Alvey Programme, UK, Professor Jean-Claude Latombe, IMAG, France, Professor Erik Sandewall, Linköping University, Sweden, William Teather, British Airways, UK, John Hubert, Unilever, Netherlands, Steven Shwartz, Cognitive Systems, USA, Daniel Sagalowicz, Framentec, Monaco, Dr Jeremy Bray, MP, Hervé Gallaire, European Computer-Industry Research Centre (ECRC), F.R. Germany, Palle Smidt, Microelectronics & Computer Technology Corporation (MCC), USA, Hermann Hauser, Acorn Computers, and my colleagues David Brandin and Joel Johnson.

Thanks are also due to Fiona Bewers, Jo Fazackerley, Shirley Gunnell, Mary Hall, Joan Smith and Kay Stephensmith for their work in organising the conference, and preparing this record. We are also indebted to Ernest Kirkwood and Peter Jackson of Cambridge University Press for their assistance with its publication. Finally, particular thanks are due to Ian Benson without whose energy and application this occasion would not have been possible.

Gordon A. England,
Executive Director,
SRI International – Europe, Middle East & Africa

April 1985

1

IAN BENSON
Introduction

> It is indeed, as Whitehead once remarked, "no accident that an age of science has developed into an age of organisation. Organised thought is the basis of organised action", not, one is tempted to add, because thought is the basis of action but rather because modern science as "the organisation of thought" introduced an element of action into thinking. Arendt (1958)

The concept of *intelligent machinery*, as proposed by Alan Turing, a Cambridge mathematician, has proved to be influential in science, technology, the economy and politics (Turing 1948). Indeed, it may be regarded as one of our major contemporary cultural landmarks. In this book we will examine aspects of the scientific progress which has been stimulated by Turing's vision. We will be particularly concerned with the state of the art in several techniques which draw their inspiration and in some cases even their domain of application from the same intellectual tradition that nurtured Turing – the tradition of formal reasoning.

Before embarking on this exercise it is perhaps useful to ask how these new techniques might relate to the evolution of computer science itself, since great claims have been, and are being, made, about the revolutionary nature of these developments. Concern with technique is of course only a part of what science is about. Kristen Nygaard has noted how a science may be regarded as related to the study of four aspects of some particular class of phenomena, of which technique, or technology, is only one. These aspects may be viewed as:

Phenomenology. The empirical study of the phenomena – their identification, observed behaviour, and properties. (Tycho Brahe in astronomy, Linnaeus in botany).

Analysis. Comprehension and explanation of phenomena in terms of an underlying theory. Identification of what are important properties and concepts, relations between properties and concepts, description of behaviour. (Newton on Physics, Darwin in biology).

Synthesis, construction, technology. Knowledge organised for the purpose of interfering with, constructing, or generating phenomena. (Teller in nuclear physics).

Multi-perspective reflection. The consideration and examination of concepts and phenomena at the same time – or alternatingly – from the perspective of more than one science, or from one or more perspective within the same science. The study of how changes introduced according to one perspective affects properties of the phenomena when regarded from another perspective. (Nygaard and Sörgaard 1985)

Nygaard has drawn attention to the development of disciplines such as botany, astronomy or physics which ultimately produced technologies built upon solid bodies of analysis, derived in turn from very extensive platforms of empirical knowledge. This might be called a "top down" process of evolution.

He notes that in contrast computer science shares with chemistry a "bottom up" pattern of development. The origin of computing, like chemistry, can be traced to rather unsuccessful attempts at construction. This is illustrated in Figure 1.1 based on Peter Wegner's outline history of computing concepts, which shows the major pre-occupations of computer scientists and their precursors from the 19th century (Wegner 1984).

The period until the sixties can be regarded as concerned almost solely with the construction of machines. In the sixties and seventies attention turned towards analysis in an attempt to identify appropriate concepts and relationships to describe the behaviour of computer based systems. Out of this attention have flowed several more or less formal system development methods and design techniques.

There is still much work to be done, however, in defining the nature of the information phenomena which lie at the heart of the study of computer science. In practical terms too narrow a focus of interest, too exclusive a concern with the techniques of software tool and machine building, often leads to unsatisfactory results. The literature is full of references to system development which is aborted, overrun, inflexible and in other ways unsatisfactory. What emerges from our review of the state of the art is that the focus of concern in computer science is shifting from direct fabrication

Figure 1.1: History of computing concepts

	Unsuccessful construction
19th cent.	Analytical Engine
	Functional abstraction
1940	Von Neumann machine Machine language and ingenious programming
1950	Numerical computation, FORTRAN
	Data abstraction
1960	Program and data structures, ALGOL, PASCAL, operating systems, timesharing object-oriented programming, SIMULA
1970	Software engineering, data abstraction Logic programming, PROLOG
1980	Interface technology; *Hardware interface technology* Fourth generation computer systems: APOLLO, PERQ Bit map displays, multiple windows, Graphic interfaces *Software interface technology* Modules, data abstractions, separation of specification and implementation, Ada emphasising software interface technology
	Knowledge abstraction
1990	Knowledge engineering from sequential to interactive, e.g. electronic books, automatic programming, expert systems, natural language interfaces, Japanese Fifth Generation Project

questions to the more or less conscious study of the phenomenology of information systems which are today complex networks of
people, machines and information processing equipment, linked
together by both human and electronic communication. This shift is
a sign of growing maturity in computer science, and has great
promise.

1.1   The formation of the research agenda

It was with this broad perspective in mind that the Cambridge conference brought together vendors and users of computer
equipment with those in the public sector concerned with the
formation of research agenda and infrastructures.

The identification of a framework for long term research has
occupied major sections of the computer science community in
recent years. Some hint of the relationship between the national
programmes as they emerged in the period 1981–83 can be seen from
Figure 1.2. This table shows how the Japanese computer science
community spent the years 1979 and '80 in a systematic study of the
state of the art at the main, largely US, centres for computing
research. They then drew up a challenging ten year research
programme to develop what they called the Fifth Generation
Computer System (FGCS), and established the Institute for New
Generation Computer Technology (ICOT) to carry it out. (JIPDEC
1981)

UK government and industry were invited by the Japanese to
attend the launch of their Fifth Generation Programme in the
autumn of 1981. The UK delegates' report led directly to the
establishment of a committee under the chairmanship of John Alvey,
Technology Director of British Telecom, charged by the government
with reporting within 9 months on an appropriate response for the
UK to the Japanese offer of participation in their programme.
Around the same time the EEC Commission proposed to the Council
of Ministers a European scientific and technical strategy for information technology (ESPRIT) to cover the period 1984–87. The
Commission's proposal, accepted by the Council in December 1982,
enabled an initial 16 pilot projects to be started in 1983. Their
proposals were given a significant boost when major European
corporations wrote to Vice President Davignon in early 1983
expressing the view that "most of the current IT industry could
disappear in a few years' time", in the absence of a co-operative
industrial programme of "sufficient magnitude".

Further European initiatives followed, notably Germany ($1bn), and Holland ($200m) in 1984.

Figure 1.2: The origin of the research agenda

Time	Japan	UK	EEC	USA
1979				
1980	Committee for Study and Research on Fifth Generation systems			
1981	Preliminary Report (fall)	Govt–Industry delegation to Japan (fall)		Software Engineering Study
1982	ICOT established ($500m committed)	Alvey Report	16 ESPRIT Pilots authorised ($11m)	DoD Software Initiative (fall)
1983		Alvey Directorate established ($500m committed). IKBS Architecture Study	Corporate endorsement: 36 ESPRIT Pilots initiated	MCC and ECRC founded
1984	Basic sequential inference machine unveiled (fall)	7 project definition studies ($1m). Agreement on UK–Japanese cooperation in Fifth Generation R&D	ESPRIT established ($1.5bn committed). First annual Workplan	Dod Strategic Computing Programme ($600m committed).

These events somewhat overtook the review of software research needs taking place in the United States. This has been undertaken for the Department of Defence (DoD) by a group of volunteer software technologists following an informal meeting at the International Conference on Software Engineering in March 1981. The strategy for a DoD software initiative was ultimately published, following several public iterations, in October 1982. It called for the DoD to mount a major programme, to be called STARS (Software Technology for Adaptable, Reliable Systems) akin to their $200m Very High Speed

Figure 1.3: Boehm's growth stages in the computer industry

Stage/decade	New shared infrastructure	Value-added issues
I 1950	None	Shared utilities Standards media
II 1960	Shared utilities and media Standard algorithms	Middle and high order languages Mixed peripherals I/O standards
III 1970	High order languages Vendor utilities I/O standards	Software unbundling Stable OS interface
IV 1980	Vendor specific OS, and utilities Plug-compatible mainframes Commercial software packages Basic software environments	Portable OS environment Networking standards

V
1990
	Ada:
	   Portable OS, utilities
	   Portable environments
	Networking standards, some main-
	frame standards
		Application standards
		Mainframe standards

VI 2000	Knowledge based application stan- dards, program generators, component libraries for some areas	Application standards for more complex knowledge domains

Integrated Circuit VLSI programme. The STARS programme proposed the establishment of a software engineering institute to spearhead the effort of diffusing Ada based technology throughout the DoD, industry and academia. According to Barry Boehm this was to be the next significant step in the evolution of the computer industry (Boehm 1983).

The Japanese project, working from much the same technical input as the DoD, had adopted a very different time scale for the rate of technical progress. In essence, they set out to bring forward a decade the development of machines anticipated by Boehm for the next century. Thus, the Japanese have gambled on changing the technological and economic base of the computer industry, leaving those with large existing investments in Ada code, or IBM mainframes, in a historical cul-de-sac.

The Japanese vision of a computer of the 1990s, as seen from the programmer's standpoint, is shown in Figure 1.4 (JIPDEC 1981). It was a far more sophisticated and challenging vision than the DoD subsequently set, although the likelihood of its achievement, like all long term research, must be open to doubt. However, one immediate consequence of the work of the Japanese, and the artificial intelligence (AI) scientists, can already be seen. An upper limit has been put on the life span of Ada as a universal language, as it was originally conceived by the DoD. As an SRI study for the US Army reported in 1980, Ada, "as it now stands or with any small set of changes, would not be suitable as a mainstream AI research language ... (while) the addition of yet more features to Ada could detract from the suitability of the language for embedded systems development" (Schwartz and Melliar-Smith 1980).

This conclusion appeared to be endorsed in 1983 when major US corporations established The Microelectronics and Computer Technology Corporation (MCC) with a goal of undertaking collaborative research in a Fifth Generation AI computer, together with software technology emphasising the use of such intelligent systems in forging a new relationship between the user and the programmer. Similar moves led to the establishment by three major European corporations of the European Computer Industry Research Centre (ECRC).

The DoD finally conceded to the new research themes by launching its Strategic Computing Programme in 1984, to develop AI applications such as autonomous vehicles, expert associates, and large scale battle management systems.

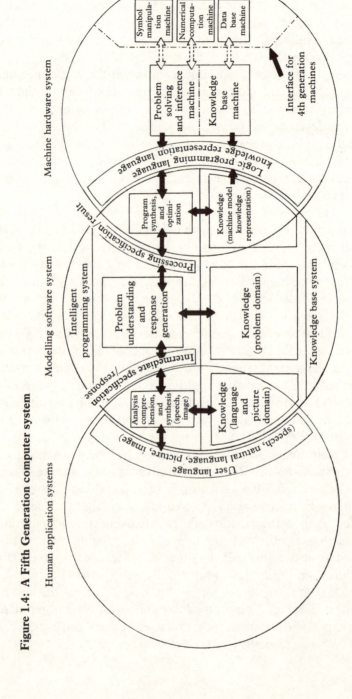

Figure 1.4: A Fifth Generation computer system

1.2 The state of the art

Artificial intelligence and software technology are now regarded as central to the research agenda of the various national research programmes. A series of six essays based on the papers read to the conference set out research directions in these key areas. They take a common perspective of logic based or symbolic computation, and look at the implications of the techniques which flow from it. The relationship between these Chapters is indicated schematically in Figure 1.5.

The earlier essays assume a basic knowledge of first-order logic and resolution which may be obtained from a book such as Nilsson

Figure 1.5: Interdependencies between research themes

(a) The role of logic in intelligent systems

(b) Natural language processing

(c) System development environments

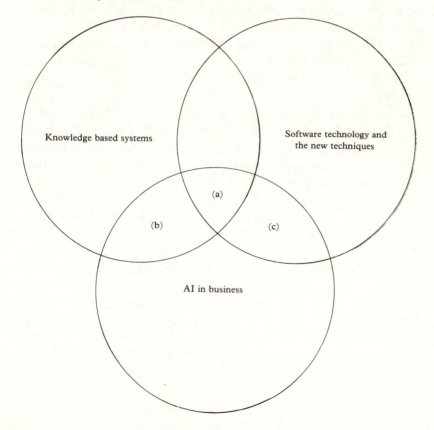

(1980). Formal logic has played an important part in artificial intelligence research for almost thirty years, but its role has always been controversial. Robert Moore's paper, Chapter 3, surveys three possible applications of logic in AI:

▶ As an analytical tool
▶ As a knowledge representation formalism and method of reasoning.
▶ As a programming language.

His essay examines each of these in turn exploring both the problems and the prospects for the successful application of logic. It provides the focus for the three overview chapters which look at knowledge based systems, software technology and AI in business. Thomas Garvey in Chapter 5 looks at the design of contempory knowledge based systems, and identifies their weaknesses, and areas for future research. In Chapter 6 Michael Melliar-Smith generalises from the experience of software and hardware design specification and verification techniques, based on theorem proving, to look at projects for semi-automatic intelligent assistants in other specialist areas, such as economic modelling. Chapter 8 on AI in Business looks at the state of the art in the application of artificial intelligence in industry, the factors affecting the take up of these techniques, and the cultural revolution in system development methods which they herald.

Two further chapters look in detail at case studies. Stanley Rosenschein, in Chapter 4, looks at the area of knowledge based systems concerned with natural language processing, to examine the various roles that logic might play in building natural language front-ends to complex systems. In Chapter 7 Erik Sandewall looks at how a synthesis of knowledge engineering and traditional software engineering might be brought about, based on a case study of the design of office automation systems.

1.3   The challenge of collaborative research

The remainder of the book records the contents of the various conference panel sessions concerned with assessing the strengths and limitations of the new research programmes and infrastructures. Particular attention was given to identifying the role of the new pre-competitive research institutions such as ICOT, ECRC and MCC in developing technologies to improve the information base for decision making.

The Editor is grateful for the assistance of Richard Ennals in reporting these seminars in his Chapters 2 and 9 which deal with research perspectives, national strategies, and the new research infrastructures. While we have endeavoured to faithfully represent the contributions made by participants, the responsibility for any errors and omissions rests with the Editor.

1.4   Conclusions

The book describes major technical, social and economic investments which have been made in initiatives for collaborative software research. We hope that it will be of value to all those who wish to make informed interventions in the processes of conception, evaluation and implementation of these unique programmes.

References and suggestions for further reading

Arendt, H. (1958). *The Human Condition*. Chicago: University of Chicago.

Boehm, B.W. (1983). Software technology in the 1990s. *IEEE Computer* 11 /83.

Nilsson, N.J. (1980). *Principles of Artificial Intelligence*. Palo Alto, California: Tioga.

JIPDEC. (1981). *Preliminary Report on Study and Research on Fifth Generation Computers*. Tokyo: Japan Information Processing Development Centre.

Nygaard & Sörgaard, (1985). Unpublished manuscript, revised version of Nygaard, K. & Haandlykken, P. (1981). The system development process – its setting, some problems and needs for methods. In *Software Engineering Environments: Proceedings of the Symposium held in Lautenbach, FRG, June 16–20, 1980*. Ed. H. Hünke. Amsterdam: North-Holland.

Schwartz, R.L. & Melliar-Smith, P.M. (1980). On the suitability of Ada for Artificial Intelligence applications. SRI Project Report 1019.

Turing, A. (1948). *Intelligent Machinery*. London: National Physical Laboratory.

Wegner, P. (1984). Capital intensive software technology. *IEEE Software*.

2

RICHARD ENNALS

Research perspectives and national strategies

2.1 Introduction

Research in advanced information technology has become a matter for general concern in recent years. Combined with the enormous increase in computer power, the sudden fall in costs brought about by the development of microcomputers has meant that computer use is now within the reach of the ordinary citizen of an advanced nation. Applications that had previously been thought to be in the domain of science fiction are discussed by computer scientist and layman alike. The veil of mystery and secrecy that partly protected the high priests of computer science from outside scrutiny has begun to be pulled aside. Issues of research perspectives and national strategy are now recognised to be worthy of discussion by politicians and industrialists. When the accompanying new infrastructures for research and development are considered, as they will be in Chapter 9 in this book, the context of discussion broadens to include potentially all citizens participating in a democracy.

This chapter draws on the contributions made by speakers at the Cambridge conference. It also seeks to broaden the discussion in the light of subsequent events, and of points of view which were not represented in Cambridge. The area of research perspectives and national strategies combines issues of politics, economics and science. We must not expect to find universal agreement, but the events of recent years have brought us nearer to consensus: not on the answers, but as to the questions that are worth asking.

2.2   Continuity in computer science

Many of the technical issues are not new. Professor Roger Needham has been at the Computer Laboratory of Cambridge University since 1956, and stated:

> It is fashionable to think that the information technology scene is in some very fundamental ways different now from what it was a rather small number of years ago. There is said to be such a thing as a Fifth Generation Computer. I have never seen one.

Needham likes to emphasise the continuity of work in computer science:

> If you look at what goes on, there is indeed a pretty good degree of continuity with the past at all points, but nevertheless there have been changes which taken together can be regarded as very serious.
>
> It is not as if somebody has made an invention which changes the face of the world, it is a conjunction of things that have happened separately.

2.3   Changing emphases in new generation computer science

The peace and tranquillity of the computing world was rudely disturbed in the autumn of 1981 by the arrival of invitations to attend a conference in Japan on the proposed development of a new generation of computers.

The Japanese were determined to set the lead in the next stage of developments in computer science, rather than continuing to be subordinate to American academic and commercial direction. They proposed an explicit scientific revolution in contrast to previous minor design changes in computer technology. The proposals were spelt out in a May 1982 publication of the Japanese Institute for New Generation Computer Technology (ICOT):

> The changes from one generation to the next in computer technology have so far been made to accommodate changes in device technology, that is from vacuum tubes to transistors,

then integrated circuits, and recently to large-scale integrated circuits. Such hindsight tells us, then, that there have been no major changes in the basic design philosophy and utilisation objectives of computers.

With fifth generation computers, however, the expected generational change is more like a "generic change" which involves not only a change in device technology, to very large scale integrated circuits (VLSI), but also simultaneous changes in design philosophy and in fields of application.

A new approach to the use of computers was proposed for a number of application fields in the 1990s, involving a change from machines centred around numerical computations to machines that can:

> assess the meaning of information and understand the problems to be solved.

To accomplish this change a number of developments are required; in the words of the ICOT report:

Figure 2.1: Organisation of the Fifth Generation Project

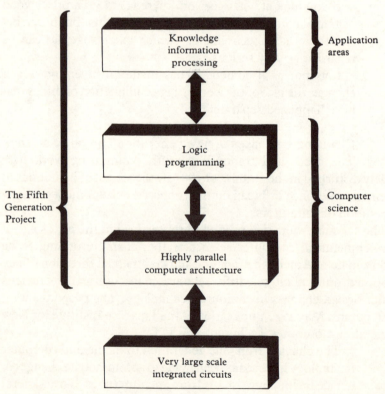

1. To realise basic mechanisms for inference, association and learning in hardware and make them the core functions of the fifth generation computers.
2. To prepare basic artificial intelligence software to fully utilise the above functions.
3. To take advantage of pattern recognition and artificial intelligence research achievements, and realise man–machine interfaces that are natural to man.
4. To realise support systems for resolving the "software crisis" and enhancing software production.

Dr Kazuhiro Fuchi is director of ICOT. In his paper "Aiming for knowledge information processing systems", published in 1981, he was explicit about the central thrust of the Japanese initiative, which he summarised in Figure 2.1.

Logic programming and its research tradition were assigned a central role in hardware and software terms:

> PROLOG (PROgramming in LOGic) seems to be the best suited as the starting point in considering new base languages for knowledge information processing.

> PROLOG machines could represent the first step toward inference machines.

Fuchi, while emphasising the radical nature of their strategy, also acknowledged the continuity with past research traditions:

> While the route to knowledge information processing is an advance to a new age, it can also be viewed as representing the inheritance and development of the legacies of the past from the viewpoint of research efforts.

Significant among the research traditions on which Fuchi and his colleagues have drawn has been that of work at Stanford Research Institute, where some of the ICOT team were visitors in the research study stage of the project. Not only did they work there on expert systems, but it was through SRI that the first copy of PROLOG reached Japan. In the chapters by SRI researchers which follow an emphasis on logic will be noted, rather than on logic programming, and LISP remains as their dominant artificial intelligence programming language.

2.4 Responses to the Japanese initiative

Professor Needham was the sole academic representative on the British Alvey Committee which was formed to consider a British response to the Japanese Fifth Generation initiative in 1981, and the invitation to British researchers to collaborate. The Japanese presentation of a considered national strategy provided a model for others to follow or reject. Whether or not inventions are involved which "change the face of the world", we must accept that, in the words of Bob Muller of SPL-Insight:

> At the very least, Japan has set the world computing targets for the rest of the decade and beyond.

In the early years of the Japanese programme, there was some confusion among overseas researchers as to the research perspective adopted by the Japanese. There was sufficient respect for the Japanese national strategy in other areas of economic and technical endeavour for governments and companies to be spurred into initiating their own programs of research and development. Unsurprisingly, research groups deployed the Japanese initiative as an argument to secure improved funding for their own preferred perspectives. At the time of the submission of the Alvey report to the British Government, Professor Max Bramer observed (Bramer 1984):

> Although the envisaged fifth generation is not a continuous development from the previous four, there is much substance to the claim that it arises naturally from existing research into Artificial Intelligence. The difference is that, whereas the Japanese project will be well-funded and nationally organised and supported, Artificial Intelligence work in the West is usually carried out in small and badly-funded research groups, especially in universities, with little or no national co-ordination. It is possible that, largely as a result of the Japanese proposals, this position may now change.

Over three years have passed since the Japanese initiative. New national research programmes have been established in most developed countries, in both East and West. They have not solely concentrated on Artificial Intelligence, nor have they all preserved the Japanese central emphasis on logic programming. One purpose of this chapter is to assess how the different programmes have progressed, starting with a review of progress on the Japanese Fifth Generation programme.

2.5   Progress in the initial stage of the Fifth Generation Programme

At the Cambridge conference reports were given by Kinji Takei, Managing Researcher in the Research Planning Department at ICOT, and Professor Hideo Aiso, Chairman of the Technology Forecasting Committee at ICOT. Further reports were given at the Fifth Generation Computer Systems conference in Tokyo later in 1984, planned as the culmination of the initial stage of the project. The overall plan is summarised in Figure 2.2:

Takei described progress as being more rapid than expected in the research and development efforts that have taken a practical approach, but rather slower in those that have chosen a more sophisticated course. This judgement would be accepted by most of the delegates at the Tokyo conference, where there was a lack of surprise at what was demonstrated – a lack of surprise due to the openness with which work in progress has been discussed.

At the end of the initial stage ICOT was able to demonstrate the new personal sequential inference machine (PSI); an enhanced version of PROLOG (KL0) (the first of a planned series of kernel languages for Fifth Generation systems); their prototype relational database machine (DELTA); and a series of example expert systems on the PSI. The work of ICOT is broader than expert systems or Artificial Intelligence, but expert systems are among the earliest demonstrable applications. One, called LOOKS, was developed with Tokyo University as a medical system to diagnose glaucoma. Another system , from Fujitsu, automates the design process of integrated circuits from a given set of specifications. A Harmoniser system arranges a four-part chorus based on a given melody.

Aiso described the project as being on course so far. He emphasised the importance of developments with PROLOG:

> PROLOG is becoming very popular in Japan among computer scientists and it seems to be that PROLOG has grown up to a new culture in Japanese computer scientists, alongside LISP. Many researchers are proposing new ideas on the language and PROLOG machines.

Figure 2.2: The FGCS plan

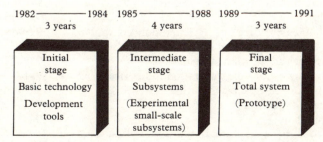

| 1982 ———— 1984 | 1985 ———— 1988 | 1989 ———— 1991 |
| 3 years | 4 years | 3 years |

Initial stage	Intermediate stage	Final stage
Basic technology	Subsystems	Total system
Development tools	(Experimental small-scale subsystems)	(Prototype)

The intermediate stage is clearly going to be difficult, designing computational models, basic architectures and algorithms, and building basic subsystems. Aiso sees the final stage as being devoted to improving and enhancing the results obtained in the previous stages, and integrating them to form a knowledge information processing system.

In recent months ICOT researchers have been at pains to point out the limits of their aspirations over the timescale of the project. Aiso said in Cambridge:

> In my opinion, it will be almost impossible to realise such an ideal knowledge information processing system in ten years. So the present Fifth Generation computer project should be devoted to basic technology required for future knowledge information processing systems.

Furthermore, although it is envisaged that future machines should have graphics, image devices and voice recognition, these are not the concern of the Fifth Generation project, which is merely one of many government-coordinated research and development projects, based on long-term planning. It is almost impossible, in Aiso's view, to "expect drastic and sophisticated evolution or breakthroughs in a short term project".

At the Tokyo conference Aiso chaired a panel discussion on "Parallelism in New Generation Computing", an issue central to the development of a new computer technology. Ehud Shapiro, of the Weizmann Institute in Israel and a regular visitor to ICOT, warned that the development of parallel computing would not be easier than that of sequential computers. All the important machine-dependent concepts of computer science have to be rediscovered in a new context. In the existing technology both computers and program-

Figure 2.3: Japanese national projects for future computer technology

Very-high-performance computer systems	1966–1971
Pattern information processing systems	1971–1980
VLSI technology	1976–1979
Basic technologies for Fourth Generation computer systems	1979–1983
Optoelectronics application system	1979–1986
Basic technologies for next generation industries	1981–1990
Very-high-speed scientific computing systems	1981–1988
Fifth Generation computer systems	1982–1991
Intelligent robots	1984–1991

mers are too slow, and although a parallel machine with an appropriate language could provide the solution the perspective is clearly long-term.

2.6 The European Strategic Programme for Research and Development in Information Technologies (ESPRIT) – progress report

At the Cambridge conference a report on the ESPRIT programme was given by Horst Hünke, who is in charge of Programme Coordination in the Directorate for Information Technology and ESPRIT of the Commission of the European Communities. Since that conference there have been further developments such as the publication of the 1985 ESPRIT workplan, approval of further projects, and public discussions of the complementarity of the ESPRIT and individual national programmes.

Hünke stated the case for ESPRIT very much in economic terms:

> Overall there is a need for ESPRIT because the leading companies' activities are much smaller than those of overseas companies, and their revenue in a number of cases can clearly not support the necessary research and development. Whilst also in the internal markets, the foreign controlled and foreign owned companies are very important. That is, they further reduce the home base for the companies for which they could produce products that can then successfully compete on the world market.

He described the historical context whereby the centre of innovative activity, which used to be in Europe in the nineteenth and early twentieth centuries, had now moved to the United States and Japan. He cited the problem of a shortage of skilled manpower (to which we will return in Chapter 9), which compounded with the consequences of being organised in small separate nation-states means that on a European level duplication of efforts cannot really be afforded. At present European industry was developing products with too low a level of technology.

The problem was broader than that of industrial research and development, for there was also an application lag, in that users are more conservative in their habits of buying equipment than in the USA.

The ESPRIT programme addresses the area of pre-competitive research, aiming to build a technological base that will make it competitive on the world market within the next five to ten years.

Hünke's analysis of American programmes in the field suggested that those that were especially successful not only initiated a technology push, but also provided an initial market, so that then the normal industrial market forces took over. A similar process would be required in Europe.

Although one of the stimuli for the ESPRIT programme has been the Japanese Fifth Generation initiative, Hünke was at pains to emphasise how the ESPRIT programme differed:

> It is not, as for instance the Japanese program is, focused along one idea, namely the Fifth Generation Computer System... The idea of the Fifth Generation computer is not a goal, but rather it is a means to focus thought. What you can see in the Fifth Generation programme, is the use of PROLOG as a basic paradigm. This is, of course, a very useful thing in providing a common semantic basis for people doing research. They understand each other's problems much more easily than if they all followed a different school.

The ESPRIT work programme does not adopt such common paradigms, and the interests of the researchers are more diverse.

Whereas the Japanese Fifth Generation project, like other advanced research projects in Japan, is organised by the Ministry of International Trade and Industry (MITI), and coordinated by the specialist Electro-Technical Laboratory (ETL), collaboration in ESPRIT is much looser. To quote Hünke:

> The ESPRIT programme is the organisation of a process of collaboration, between industrial partners, between industry and academia; a process that is mediated but not run in that sense by the Commission. It is strongly influenced by its participants.

A recent survey of the ESPRIT programme (*fgcs Journal*, Vol 1, No. 1, July 1984) made the contrast in terms of research strategies:

> Whereas the Japanese MITI directs research and development within an overall strategy, ESPRIT and other programmes merely back industry proposals.

The area covered by the work programme, which itself constitutes an invitation to make proposals, is much broader than that covered by the Japanese Fifth Generation project. ESPRIT seeks to remedy a wider range of research and development deficiencies, and includes areas covered by other Japanese projects. Figure 2.4 is the outline of the programme taken from the 1985 Workplan:

The area with which we are most concerned is that of "Advanced Information Processing" (AIP). This is described in the Workplan as follows:

This subprogramme is seeking means for improving the performance and efficiency of computing systems by making use of advances in four key areas, namely, knowledge

Figure 2.4: The ESPRIT programme

---

1. Subprogramme 1: Advanced microelectronics
   R & D areas
   1.1 Submicron MOS
   1.2 Submicron bipolar
   1.3 Computer Aided Design (CAD)
   1.4 Compound semiconductor integrated circuits
   1.5 Optoelectronics
   1.6 Advanced display technologies

2. Subprogramme 2: Software technology
   R & D areas
   2.1 Theories, methods and tools
   2.2 Management and industrial aspects
   2.3 Common environment

3. Subprogramme 3: Advanced information processing
   R & D areas
   3.1 Knowledge engineering
   3.2 External interfaces
   3.3 Information and knowledge storage
   3.4 Computer architectures
   3.5 Design and systems aspects
   3.6 Focusing projects

4. Subprogramme 4: Office systems
   R & D areas
   4.1 Office systems science and human factors
   4.2 Advanced workstations
   4.3 Communication systems
   4.4 Advanced filing and retrieval systems
   4.5 Integrated office system

5. Subprogramme 5: Computer integrated manufacture
   R & D areas
   5.0 Manufacturing company strategy and organisation
   5.1 Integrated system architecture
   5.2 Computer Aided Design and Engineering (CAD/CAE)
   5.3 Computer Aided Manufacturing (CAM)
   5.4 Machine control systems
   5.5 Subsystems and components
   5.6 CIM systems applications

---

engineering, including the development of knowledge acquisition, representation and manipulation techniques; external interfaces, dealing with the recognition, understanding and synthesis of signals; information and knowledge storage. These advances are the developments in data and knowledge bases as well as the techniques of access to these bases, and deals with architectural characteristics and physical properties of advanced storage devices; computer architecture, i.e. the development of new computer architectures and their associated programming environments where particular emphasis will be placed on the use of concurrency.

The ESPRIT programme was approved by the EEC Council of Ministers for an initial period of five years in February 1984, and 120 projects were under way by the end of 1984. Each proposal must come from a consortium made up of at least two companies from different member states, with research and higher education institutions able to participate. Successful proposals receive 50% funding.

It is too early to judge the technical outcomes of the ESPRIT programme, but it is worth noting that PROLOG, the language adopted by the Japanese as their principal paradigm, was first implemented and developed in Europe. Researchers in logic programming, and in artificial intelligence in general, have had little funding for their work until recently, and a small but influential European academic community has developed for mutual support, some of whom have taken temporary residence in the United States.

2.7   The United Kingdom Alvey Programme in advanced information technology – a progress report

The Alvey Programme was represented at the Cambridge conference by its Director, Brian Oakley. He drew attention to the similarities between the Alvey strategy and that of ESPRIT and the Japanese Fifth Generation Project. Referring to technical directions, he said:

> You could just scratch out the bit which says "ESPRIT" and write in "Alvey" and nobody would notice the difference in many ways.

Concerning the general approach to research planning, he said:

> The Alvey programme is quite unashamedly copying what we see as the best features of the Japanese programme as well as we can in transplanting it to the British scene. This is particularly true of the administrative arrangements. In

many ways, when we wonder what to do, we look up the Japanese Fifth Generation plans and then we see how to organise ourselves. Let me assure you that to copy in Europe is recognised as an extreme form of flattery.

The Alvey programme was set up in 1983 following the British government's acceptance of the majority of the recommendations of the Alvey Committee (chaired by John Alvey of British Telecom). Whereas in Japan MITI coordinated the work of eight collaborating companies focused on the ICOT research centre, in the United Kingdom the Alvey Directorate coordinates a much wider collaborative programme. Three government ministries are involved (the Department of Trade and Industry, the Ministry of Defence, and the Science and Engineering Research Council of the Department of Education and Science), together with industry and academic research groups.

Like the ESPRIT programme, the Alvey programme is broader and less focused than the Fifth Generation project. It is concerned with the development of what are described as the four crucial enabling technologies for advanced information technology:

> Very Large Scale Integration (VLSI)
> Software Engineering
> Man–Machine Interface (MMI)
> Intelligent Knowledge Based Systems (IKBS)

The directorate is organised into corresponding sections, though as Oakley concedes:

> the distinction between the areas is no more than a device that human beings use to try to administer such things.

He noted, however, that there do appear to have been barriers between academic communities with apparently related interests:

> It does seem to us to be very important to try to bring these communities together. It is a strange thing that they inter-mingle so closely, and yet the barriers between them are really very extreme. It's terribly easy, I find, to say a man belongs to the AI community or he belongs to the software engineering community. It is remarkably difficult to find the people who cross these two communities.

It may be useful to outline the work of the different sections of the Alvey programme, in summary form:

VLSI. Work has been led by the large computer manufacturers, and concerns:

▶ silicon whole-process development
cmos
bi-polar
silicon on insulator
1.5 micron features in year 3
1.0 micron features in year 5
▶ equipment for same
▶ CAD for VLSI standard design codes
▶ silicon brokerage to serve immediate needs of smaller companies

Man–machine interface. This section represents an uneasy coalition of the concerns of previously separate academic communities, and deals with i.e.:

▶ speech recognition
▶ pattern analysis
▶ ergonomics
▶ better displays
▶ links with cognitive sciences, psychology, etc.

Software engineering. This part of the Alvey programme builds most explicitly on the methods of conventional computer science. It is an area given relatively little emphasis in Japan, where the view is that new software technology should overcome many current software problems. British companies have been somewhat reluctant to make the investment in software engineering research under Alvey or ESPRIT. Work has concentrated on the production of Integrated Programming Support Environments:

▶ First Generation
    File-based tool set
    Unix
▶ Second Generation
    Database-based tool set
    Distributed Operating System
    Formal Specification Methods
▶ Third Generation
    IKBS-based tool set

IKBS. The IKBS area has had the greatest academic contribution, and much of the strategy stems from an SERC working party which preceded the Alvey Report. It is organised around the following research themes:

▶ Parallel Architectures
▶ Declarative Languages
▶ Intelligent Data Base Systems
▶ Expert Systems
▶ Intelligent Front Ends
▶ Inference
▶ Natural Language
▶ Image Interpretation
▶ Intelligent Computer-aided Instruction

Apart from projects in the separate areas, a number of large "demonstrator" projects were established, drawing on the different enabling technologies, such as a project for knowledge based decision support with the Department of Health and Social Security, two companies and three universities; and a voice-driven desktop workstation, exploiting new parallel computer architecture and work in phonetics and linguistics, involving two companies, three universities and an associated research consortium.

According to figures cited by Oakley at the September conference, 93 projects had been approved from 274 proposals. There were an average of 4.3 partners per project. A total of 45 companies, 38 universities, 4 polytechnics and 5 other establishments were involved. Further projects were to be approved before the spring of 1985, leading to 80% of the budget being committed. The majority of contracts went to large companies, and ten leading universities were the academic partners in over half of the projects.

There were increasing complaints in the early part of the programme along the lines of "Where is the Fifth Generation in the Alvey Programme?" In the summer of 1984 an initiative was launched in Declarative Systems Architecture, administered through the IKBS section but underlying the whole programme. This focused attention on parallel architectures such as the ALICE machine at Imperial College, to be made initially from a delta network of Inmos transputers. A Compiler Target Language (CTL) was agreed for the implementation of declarative languages. New programmes were launched in large knowledge bases and in logic programming languages, applications and architectures.

Brian Oakley is reluctant to make mid-term assessments of the progress of the programme:

> The proof of the pudding is in the eating. It is no damn good, really, taking the pudding out of the oven and having a look to see how it is getting on at this stage.

2.8   A brief survey of national strategies in other countries

The United States. In the United States the Defence Advanced Research Projects Agency (DARPA) has launched a Strategic Computing Programme, with a budget of $600m over five years. The main demand has come from the military, with artificial intelligence applications such as autonomous vehicles, expert associates, and large-scale battle management systems.

IBM has taken an increasing interest in Fifth Generation Computer Systems and logic programming, having been publicly dismissive at the time of the Japanese initiative. They have been recruiting leading international researchers in logic programming for their Yorktown Heights research centre.

In response to the perceived threats from both Japan and IBM, eighteen computer manufacturers have united to form the Microelectronics and Computing Technology Centre (MCC) based in Austin, Texas, which will be discussed further in Chapter 9. This necessitated changes in the existing anti-trust legislation in the 1984 Joint Research and Development Act.

West Germany. Following the 1984 Riesenhuber report on Information Technology, a programme of $1bn over five years has been established, placing a special emphasis on co-operation between research establishments and industry in order to achieve a faster application of research and development results to new products. Research was to be encouraged in knowledge engineering, new computer structures, and CAD for computers and software.

In addition to participation in the ESPRIT programme, West Germany is host to the new European Computer Industry Research Centre (ECRC) in Munich, involving Siemens, Bull and ICL, which will be discussed further in Chapter 9.

France. In France, research and development initiatives relating to the facets of the Fifth Generation programme appear as a set of distinct projects that complement each other technically as well as in their scientific and industrial objectives. Government felt that the French Information Technology industry should master the full range of technologies, and in 1983 initiated seven major technology transfer projects. These complement a series of Joint Research Projects in fields such as advanced programming, various facets of Artificial Intelligence, and concurrency, co-operation and communication.

The Soviet Union and Eastern Europe. Recent reports suggest that the Soviet Union is planning a "low budget" fifth generation programme along similar lines to those in Japan, the United Kingdom or the United States. The Communist countries intend to leapfrog our present fourth generation computers from the third generation of computers which they now employ. This is to be part of the third computing (five year) plan.

The Soviet Commission for Computer Engineering (CCE), based at the Moscow Academy of Sciences, has agreed the five principal goals of the plan:

▶ very large scale integration microprocessors for storage and processing, including fabrication techniques, to give advanced hardware
▶ parallel and multiprocessor computer architectures
▶ intelligent databases and methods of operation
▶ software methodologies
▶ logic programming basis for computer operation

A major part in the Soviet plans will be played by the Institute for Computer Coordination (SZKI) in Budapest, which was the first group to write applications programs in PROLOG, in 1977. Over 250 expert systems have been produced, for everything from running collective farms to manipulating molecules in three dimensions. In 1982 the Japanese researchers from ICOT purchased the Hungarian MPROLOG, which is available commercially in Western Europe and North America. Soviet scientists have also been taking increasing interest in this research area, as have their colleagues in Bulgaria, East Germany, Poland and Rumania.

2.9   Some notes of scepticism

A large number of national research programmes have been assembled in a very short time, and no advanced country can feel complete without one. Indeed, the spread of computing technology is such that research programmes are no longer the monopoly of advanced countries. In addition to the countries mentioned above major research centres are being established, to the author's knowledge, in Canada, Australia, Portugal, Sweden, Israel, China, Brazil and India. Is this a wise use of money and resources?

At the Cambridge conference, Dr Jeremy Bray MP expressed his unease about certain aspects of fifth generation computer developments. He looked at other areas of science, and wondered if there were not a number of unexploited scientific openings in other fields, and whether among the many projects now being refused funding by the British Science and Engineering Research Council there were not a large proportion which have better formulated problems and far less adequate resources than we are trying to marshal in the artificial intelligence field. He also questioned the concepts which at the conference were taken as points of reference: the fetch and carry robot and the personal information assistant. In his view:

> these are more in the nature of the medieval philosopher's stone than objectives in a modern Popperian science and technology. It also seems to me that they are rather inadequate conceptions of behaviour, whether individual or social.

Dr Bray had a further worry, that research programmes such as the Alvey programme were technique driven rather than application driven. This is of course implicit in the emphasis on enabling technologies. Dr Thomas Garvey to a certain extent shared his view, when he said:

> There is a phenomenon in Artificial Intelligence at least, and I suspect in computer science generally, that you start to solve a problem by first inventing a language that will enable you to express it better or quicker or whatever. It appears that what we like to do best really is to invent tools rather than necessarily solving the problems, and sometimes we have to first invent problems which will then require these tools.

We may wish to apply this analysis to Garvey's own account of Knowledge Based Systems, which is given in Chapter 5.

2.10 Conclusions

Professor Ted Elcock has observed with respect to the Fifth Generation projects that "between the expectation and the reality lies the shadow". We can describe what we want to achieve, using a declarative language such as PROLOG, but to obtain the desired outcome is less straightforward, and many technical issues remain unresolved.

We are now in the shadow. Those who are expecting quick results may well be disappointed. Serious researchers are reconciled to many years of hard work, and success is not guaranteed for all participants. This is not, in the words of Lewis Carroll, a "caucus race".

Professor Alan Robinson, now of Syracuse University but like Elcock and many others a British expatriate in North America, has reviewed the problem of research strategies in his paper "Logic programming – past, present and future", first presented at ICOT in 1983. He was the originator of the Resolution principle in 1965, preparing the way for logic programming, and is the founding editor of the *Journal of Logic Programming*. addressing his Japanese audience, he said:

> I sometimes have a twinge of anxiety about your having made logic programming the central theme in your Fifth Generation Project. I wonder whether your great confidence in this idea is going to be justified. There are some risks involved, as you well know, in putting this idea in the centre.

On the other hand, on looking to the future, he sees more hope in the Fifth Generation approach than in the traditional American approach based on expert knowledge engineers:

> I think we can expect expert systems to be in general use. Once the tools are available, I do not believe that a special kind of expert – the "knowledge engineer" – will be needed to implement such systems. The point of the Fifth Generation revolution is to eliminate, as far as possible, the role of such a go-between. Today's situation, in which the professional expert is not necessarily able to express his expertise in suitable computational form, is not the model for the future. We must expect that "logic programming literacy" will become widespread.

References and suggestions for further reading

Alvey, J. (1982). *A Programme for Advanced Information Technology. The report of the Alvey Committee*. London; HMSO.

Bramer, M. (1984). The Japanese Fifth Generation Computer Project. In *New Information Technology*, ed. A. Burns Chichester: Ellis Horwood.

Campbell, J.A. (ed.) (1984). *Iplementations of PROLOG*. chichester; Ellis Horwood.

Clark, K.L., Darlington, J., Kowalski, R.A. & Ennals J.R. (1984). Research Plan of the Declarative Systems Research Group Department of Computing. Imperial College.

Commission of the European Communities (1984). Draft Council Decision adopting the 1985 work programme for the European Strategic Programme for Research and Development in Information Technologies (ESPRIT). COM(84) 608 final.

Elcock, E.W. (1983). The Pragmatics of PROLOG. In *Proceedings of Logic Programming Workshop*, ed. L. Pereira. Lisbon: University of Lisbon.

Feigenbaum, E.A. & McCorduck, P. (1983). *The Fifth Generation*. London; Addison-Wesley.

Frederiksson, E. (1984). Overview of national strategies. *future generations computer Systems*, Vol. 1, No. 1. July 1984.

Fuchi, K. (1981). Aiming for knowledge information processing systems. Electro-

Technical Laboratory and in *Logic Programming and its Applications*, ed. D. Warren, M. Van Caneghem. San Francisco: Ablex 1984.

ICOT (1984). *Proceedings of Fifth Generation Computer Systems Conference Tokyo.* November 1984.

Kowalski, R.A. (1984). Software engineering and Artificial Intelligence in new generation computing. *Future Generations Computer systems*, Vol. 1, No. 1 July 1984.

Moto-oka, T. (ed.) (1982). *Fifth Generation Computer Systems.* Amsterdam; North-Holland.

Muller, R. (ed.) (1984). *Impact 84.* Abingdon; SPL-Insight.

Robinson, J.A (1983). Logic Programming - past, present and future. ICOT TR - 015.

Simons, G.L. (1983). *Towards Fifth-Generation Computers.* Manchester; NCC Publications.

Walton, P. (1984). An account of research strategies in the Soviet Union and Eastern Europe, with special attention to Hungary. *Computing*, 24th May 1984

3

ROBERT MOORE

The role of logic in intelligent systems

3.1   Introduction

Formal logic has played an important part in artificial intelligence (AI) research for almost thirty years, but its role has always been controversial. This paper surveys three possible applications of logic in AI: (1) as an analytical tool, (2) as a knowledge representation formalism and method of reasoning, and (3) as a programming language. The paper examines each of these in turn, exploring both the problems and the prospects for the successful application of logic.

3.2   Logic as an analytical tool

Analysis of the content of knowledge representations is the application of logic in artificial intelligence that is, in a sense, conceptually prior to all others. It has become a truism to say that, for a system to be intelligent, it must have knowledge, and currently the only way we know of for giving a system knowledge is to embody it in some sort of structure – a *knowledge representation*. Now, whatever else a formalism may be, at least some of its expressions must have *truth-conditional semantics* if it is really to be a representation of knowledge. That is, there must be some sort of correspondence between an expression and the world, such that it makes sense to ask whether the world is the way the expression claims it to be. To have knowledge at all is to have knowledge that the world is one way and not otherwise. If one's "knowledge" does not rule out any possibilities for how the world might be, then one really does not know anything at all.

⚹ Moreover, whatever AI researchers may say, examination of their practice reveals that they do rely (at least informally) on being able to provide truth-conditional semantics for their formalisms. Whether we are dealing with conceptual dependencies, frames, semantic networks, or what have you, as soon as we say that a particular piece of structure represents the assertion (or belief, or knowledge) that John hit Mary, we have hold of something that is true if John did hit Mary and false if he didn't.

Mathematical logic (particularly model theory) is simply the branch of mathematics that deals with this sort of relationship between expressions and the world. If one is going to analyze the truth-conditional semantics of a representation formalism, then, *a fortiori*, one is going to be engaged in logic. As Newell puts it, "Just as talking of programmerless programming violates truth in packaging, so does talking of a *non-logical* analysis of knowledge." (Newell 1980).

While the use of logic as a tool for the analysis of meaning is perhaps the least controversial application of logic to AI, many proposed knowledge representations have failed to pass minimal standards of adequacy in this regard. (Woods 1975 and Hayes 1977 have both discussed this point at length.) For example, Kintch (1974) suggests representing "All men die" by (DIE,MAN) & (ALL,MAN). How are we to evaluate such a proposal? Without a formal specification of how the meaning of this complex expression is derived from the meaning of its parts, all we can do is take the representation on faith. However, given some plausible assumptions, we can show that this expression cannot mean what Kintch says it does.

The assumptions we need to make are that "&" means logical conjunction (i.e., "and"), and that related sentences receive analogous representations. In particular, we will assume that any expression of the form (P & Q) is true if and only if P is true and Q is true, and that "Some men dance" ought to be represented by (DANCE,MAN) & (SOME,MAN). If this were the case, however, "All men die" and "Some men dance" taken together would imply "All men dance". That, of course, does not follow, so we have shown that, if our assumptions are satisfied, the proposed representation cannot be correct. Perhaps Kintch does not intend for "&" to be interpreted as "and", but then he owes us an explanation of what it *does* mean that is compatible with his other proposals.

Just to show that these model theoretic considerations do not simply lead to a requirement that we use standard logical notation, we can demonstrate that ALL(MAN,DIE) could be an adequate representation of "All men die". We simply let MAN denote the set of all men, let DIE denote the set of all things that die, and let ALL(X,Y) be true whenever the set denoted by X is a sub-set of the set denoted by Y. Then it will immediately follow that ALL(MEN,DIE) is true just in case all men die. Hence there is a systematic way of interpreting ALL(MEN,DIE) that is compatible with what it is claimed to mean.

The point of this exercise is that we want to be able to write computer programs whose behavior is a function of the meaning of the structures they manipulate. However, the behavior of a program can be directly influenced only by the form of those structures. Unless there is some systematic relationship between form and meaning, our goal cannot be realised.

3.3 Logic as a knowledge representation and reasoning system

The logic controversy in AI. The second major application of logic to artificial intelligence is to use logic as a knowledge representation formalism in an intelligent computer system and to use logical deduction to draw inferences from the knowledge thus represented. Strictly speaking, there are two issues here. One could imagine using formal logic in a knowledge representation system, without using logical deduction to manipulate the representations, and one could even use logical deduction on representations that have little resem-blance to standard formal logics; but the use of a logic as a representa-tion and the use of logical deduction to draw inferences from the knowledge represented fit together in such a way that it makes most sense to consider them simultaneously.

This is a much more controversial application than merely using the tools of logic to analyse knowledge representation systems. Indeed, Newell explicitly states that "the role of logic (is) as a tool for the analysis of knowledge, not for reasoning by intelligent agents" (Newell 1980). It is a commonly held opinion in the field that logic-based representations and logical deduction were tried many years ago and were found wanting. As Newell expresses it, "The lessons of the sixties taught us something about the limitations of using logics for this role." (Newell 1980).

The lessons referred to by Newell were the conclusions widely drawn from early experiments in "resolution theorem-proving". In the mid-1960s, J. A. Robinson developed a relatively simple, logically complete method for proving theorems in first-order logic, based on the so-called resolution principle:

$$(P \lor Q), (\neg P \lor R) \vdash (Q \lor R)$$

That is, if we know that either P is true or Q is true and that either P is false or R is true, then we can infer that either Q is true or R is true.

Robinson's work brought about a rather dramatic shift in attitudes regarding the automation of logical inference. Previous efforts at automatic theorem-proving were generally thought of as exercises in expert problem solving, with the domain of application being logic, geometry, number theory, etc. The resolution method, however, seemed powerful enough to be used as a universal problem solver. Problems would be formalised as theorems to be proved in first-order logic in such a way that the solution could be extracted from the proof of the theorem.

The results of experiments directed towards this goal were disappointing. The difficulty was that, in general, the search space generated by the resolution method grows exponentially (or worse) with the number of formulas used to describe the problem and with the length of the proof, so that problems of even moderate complexity could not be solved in reasonable time. Several domain-independent heuristics were proposed to try to deal with this issue, but they proved too weak to produce satisfactory results. In the reaction that followed, not only was there a turning away from attempts to use deduction to create general problem solvers, but there was also widespread condemnation of any use of logic in commonsense reasoning or problem-solving systems.

The problem of incomplete knowledge. Despite the disappointments of the early experiments with resolution, there has been a recent revival of interest in the use of logic-based knowledge representation systems and deduction-based approaches to commonsense reasoning and problem solving. To a large degree this renewed interest seems to stem from the recognition of an important class of problems that resist solution by any other method.

The key issue is the extent to which a system has complete knowledge of the relevant aspects of the problem domain and the specific situation in which it is operating. To illustrate, suppose we have a knowledge base of personnel information for a company and we want to know whether any programmer earns more than the manager of data processing. If we have recorded in our knowledge base the job title and salary of every employee, we can simply find the salary of each programmer and compare it with the salary of the manager of data processing. This sort of "query evaluation" is essentially just an extended form of table lookup. No deductive reasoning is involved.

On the other hand, we might not have specific salary information in the knowledge base. Instead, we might have only general information such as "all programmers work in the data processing department, the manager of a department is the manager of all other employees of that department, and no employee earns more than his manager". From this information, we can deduce that no programmer earns more than the manager of data processing, although we have no information about the exact salary of any employee.

A representation formalism based on logic gives us the ability to represent information about a situation, even when we do not have a complete description of the situation. Deduction-based inference methods allow us to answer logically complex queries using a knowledge base containing such information, even when we cannot "evaluate" a query directly. On the other hand, AI inference systems that are not based on automatic-deduction techniques either do not permit logically complex queries to be asked, or they answer such queries by methods that depend on the possession of complete information.

First-order logic can represent incomplete information about a situation by

Saying that something has a certain property without saying which thing has that property:

$\exists x P(x)$

Saying that everything in a certain class has a certain property without saying what everything in that class is:

$\forall x (P(x) \supset Q(x))$

Saying that at least one of two statements is true without saying which statement is true:

$(P \lor Q)$

Explicitly saying that a statement is false, as distinguished from not saying that it is true:

¬P

These capabilities would seem to be necessary for handling the kinds of incomplete information that people can understand, and thus they would be required for a system to exhibit what we would regard as general intelligence. Any representation formalism that has these capabilities will be, at the very least, an extension of classical first-order logic, and any inference system that can deal adequately with these kinds of generalizations will have to have at least the capabilities of an automatic-deduction system.

The control problem in deduction. If the negative conclusions that were widely drawn from the early experiments in automatic theorem-proving were fully justified, then we would have a virtual proof of the impossibility of creating intelligent systems based on the knowledge representation approach, since many types of incomplete knowledge that people are capable of dealing with seem to demand the use of logical representation and deductive inference. A careful analysis, however, suggests that the failure of the early attempts to do commonsense reasoning and problem solving by theorem-proving had more specific causes that can be attacked without discarding logic itself.

The point of view we shall adopt here is that there is nothing wrong with using logic or deduction *per se*, but that a system must have some way of knowing, out of the many possible inferences it could draw, which ones it *should* draw. A very simple, but nonetheless important, instance of this arises in deciding how to use assertions of the form P ⊃ Q ("P implies Q"). Intuitively, such a statement has at least two possible uses in reasoning. Obviously, one way of using P ⊃ Q is to infer Q, whenever we have inferred P. But P ⊃ Q can also be used, even if we have not yet inferred P, to suggest a way to infer Q, if that is what we are trying to do. These two ways of using an implication are referred to as *forward chaining* ("If P is asserted, also assert Q") and *backward chaining* ("To infer Q, try to infer P"), respectively. We can think of the deductive process as a bidirectional search, partly working forward from what we already know, partly working backward from what we would like to infer, and converging somewhere in the middle.

Unrestricted use of the resolution method turns out to be

equivalent to using every implication both ways, leading to highly redundant searches. Domain-independent refinements of resolution avoid some of this redundancy, but usually impose uniform strategies that may be inappropriate in particular cases. For example, often the strategy is to use all assertions only in a backward-chaining manner, on the grounds that this will at least guarantee that all the inferences drawn are relevant to the problem at hand.

The difficulty with this approach is that whether it is more efficient to use an assertion for forward chaining or for backward chaining can depend on the specific form of the assertion, or the set of assertions in which it is embedded. Consider, for instance, the following schema:

$$\forall x(P(F(x)) \supset P(x))$$

Instances of this schema include such things as:

$$\forall x(x+1 < y \supset x < y)$$
$$\forall x(\text{JEWISH}(\text{MOTHER}(x)) \supset \text{JEWISH}(x))$$

That is, a number x is less than a number y if $x+1$ is less than y; and a person is Jewish if his or her mother is Jewish.

Suppose we used an assertion of the form $\forall x(P(F(x)) \supset P(x))$ for backward chaining, as most "uniform" proof procedures would. In effect, we would have the rule, "To infer $P(x)$, try to infer $P(F(x))$". If, for instance, we were trying to infer $P(A)$, this rule would cause us to try to infer $P(F(A))$. This expression, however, is also of the form $P(x)$, so the process would be repeated, resulting in an infinite descending chain of formulas to be inferred:

$P(A)$
$P(F(A))$
$P(F(F(A)))$
$P(F(F(F(A))))$, etc.

If, on the other hand, we use the rule for forward chaining, the number of applications is limited by the complexity of the assertion that originally triggers the inference. Asserting a formula of the form $P(F(x))$ would result in the corresponding instance of $P(x)$ being inferred, but each step reduces the complexity of the formula produced, so the process terminates:

$P(F(F(A)))$
$P(F(A))$
$P(A)$

It turns out, then, that the efficent use of a particular assertion often depends on exactly what that assertion is, as well as on the context of other assertions in which it is embedded. Kowalski and

Moore illustrate this point with examples involving not only the distinction between forward chaining and backward chaining, but other control decisions as well (Kowalski 1979 and Moore 1980).

In some cases, control of the deductive process is affected by the details of how a concept is axiomatized, in ways that go beyond "local" choices such as that between forward and backward chaining. Sometimes logically equivalent formalizations can have radically different behavior when used with standard deduction techniques. For example, in the blocks world that has been used as a testbed for so much AI research, it is common to define the relation "A is ABOVE B" in terms of the primitive relation "A is (directly) ON B", with ABOVE being the transitive closure of ON. This can be done formally in at least three ways:

$$\forall x,y(\text{ABOVE}(x,y) \equiv (\text{ON}(x,y) \lor \exists z(\text{ON}(x,z) \lor \text{ABOVE}(z,y))))$$
$$\forall x,y(\text{ABOVE}(x,y) \equiv (\text{ON}(x,y) \lor \exists z(\text{ABOVE}(x,z) \lor \text{ON}(z,y))))$$
$$\forall x,y(\text{ABOVE}(x,y) \equiv (\text{ON}(x,y) \lor \exists z(\text{ABOVE}(x,z) \lor \text{ABOVE}(z,y))))$$

Each of these axioms will produce different behavior in a standard deduction system, no matter how we make such local control decisions as whether to use forward or backward chaining. The first axiom defines ABOVE in terms of ON, in effect, by iterating upward from the lower object, and would therefore be useful for enumerating all the objects that are above a given object. The second axiom iterates downward from the upper object, and could be used for enumerating all the objects that a given object is above. The third axiom, though, is essentially a "middle out" definition, and is hard to control for any specific use.

The early systems for problem solving by theorem-proving were often inefficient because axioms were chosen for their simplicity and brevity, without regard to their computational properties – a problem that also arises in conventional programming. To take a well-known example, the simplest procedure for computing the nth Fibonacci number is a doubly recursive algorithm whose execution time is proportional to 2^n, while a slightly more complicated, less intuitively defined, singly recursive procedure can compute the same function in time proportional to n.

Prospects for logic-based reasoning systems. The fact that the issues discussed in this section were not taken into account in the early experiments in problem solving by theorem-proving suggests that not too much weight should be given to the negative results that were obtained. As yet, however, there is not enough experience with providing explicit control information and manipulating the form of axioms for computational efficiency to tell whether large bodies of commonsense knowledge can be dealt with effectively through deductive techniques. If the answer turns out to be "no", then some radically new approach will be required for dealing with incomplete knowledge.

3.4   Logic as a programming language

Computation and deduction. The parallels between the manipulation of axiom systems for efficient deduction and the design of efficient computer programs were recognised in the early 1970s by a number of people, notably Hayes (1973), Kowalski (1974), and Colmerauer (1978). It was discovered, moreover, that there are ways to formalize many functions and relations so that the application of standard deduction methods will have the effect of executing them as efficient computer programs. These observations have led to the development of the field of logic programming and the creation of new computer languages such as PROLOG (Warren, Pereira and Pereira 1977).

As an illustration of the basic idea of logic programming, consider the function APPEND, which appends one list to the end of another. This function can be implemented in LISP as follows:

(APPEND A B) =
(COND ((NULL A) B)
            (T (CONS (CAR A) (APPEND (CDR A) B))))

What this function definition says is that the result of appending B to the end of A is B if A is the empty list, otherwise it is a list whose first element is the first element of A and whose remainder is the result of appending B to the remainder of A.

We can easily write a set of axioms in first-order logic that explicitly say what we just said in English. If we treat APPEND as a three-place relation (with APPEND(A,B,C) meaning that C is the result of appending B to the end of A) the axioms might look as follows:

$\forall x(\text{APPEND}(\text{NIL},x,x)$
$\forall x,y,z(\text{APPEND}(x,y,z) \supset$
            $\forall w(\text{APPEND}(\text{CONS}(w,x),y,\text{CONS}(w,z))))$

To see the equivalence between the LISP program and these axioms, note that $\text{CONS}(w,x)$ corresponds to A, so that w corresponds to (CAR A) and x corresponds to (CDR A).

The key observation is that, when these axioms are used via backward chaining to infer APPEND(A,B,x), where A and B are arbitrary lists and x is a variable, the resulting deduction process not only terminates with the variable x bound to the result of appending B to the end of A, it exactly mirrors the execution of the corresponding LISP program. This suggests that in many cases, by controlling the use of axioms correctly, deductive methods can be used to simulate ordinary computation with no loss of efficiency. The new view of the relationship between deduction and computation that emerged from these observations was, as Hayes (1973) put it, "Computation is controlled deduction".

The ideas of logic programming have produced a very exciting and fruitful new area of research. However, as with all good new ideas, there has been a degree of "over-selling" of logic programming and, particularly, of the PROLOG language. So, if the following sections focus more on the limitations of logic programming than on its strengths, they should be viewed as an effort to counterbalance some of the overstated claims made elsewhere.

Logic programming and PROLOG. To date, the main application of the idea of logic programming has been the development of the programming language PROLOG. Because it has roots both in programming methodology and in automatic theorem-proving, there is a widespread ambivalence about how PROLOG should be viewed. Sometimes it is seen as "just a programming language", although with some very interesting and useful features, and other times it is viewed as an "inference engine", which can be used directly as the basis of a reasoning system. On occasion these two ways of looking at PROLOG are simply confused, as when the (false) claim is made that to program in PROLOG one has simply to state the facts of the problem one is trying to solve and the PROLOG system will take care of everything else. This confusion is also evident in the terminology associated with the Japanese fifth generation computer project, in which the basic measure of machine speed is said to be "logical inferences per second". We will try to separate these two ways of looking at PROLOG, evaluating it first as a programming language and then as an inference system.

To evaluate PROLOG as a programming language, we will compare it with LISP, the programming language most widely used in AI. The fact that the idea of logic programming grew out of AI work on automated inference, of course, gives AI no special status as a domain of application for logic programming. But because it was developed by people working in AI, and because it provides good facilities for symbol manipulation, most PROLOG applications have been within AI.

PROLOG incorporates a number of features not found in LISP:

▶ Failure-driven backtracking
▶ Procedure invocation by pattern matching (unification)
▶ Pattern matching as a substitute for selector functions
▶ Procedures with multiple outputs
▶ Returning and passing partial results via structures containing logical variables

These features and others make PROLOG an extremely powerful language for certain applications. For example, its incorporation of backtracking, pattern matching, and logical variables make it ideal for the implementation of depth-first parsers for language processing. (This is in fact the application for which it was invented.) It is probably impossible to do this as efficiently in LISP as in PROLOG. Moreover, having pattern matching as the standard way of passing information between procedures and decomposing complex structures makes many programs much simpler to write and understand in PROLOG than in LISP. On the other hand, PROLOG lacks general purpose operators for changing data structures. In applications where such facilities are needed, such as maintaining a highly interconnected network structure, PROLOG can be awkward to use. For this type of application, using LISP is much more straightforward.

To better understand the advantages and disadvantages of PROLOG relative to LISP, it is helpful to consider that PROLOG and LISP both contain a purely declarative subset, in which every expression affects the course of a computation only by its value, not by "side effects". For example, evaluating $(2+3)$ would normally not change the computational state of the system, while evaluating $(X \leftarrow 3)$ would change the value of X. In comparing their "pure" subsets, one finds that PROLOG is strictly more general than LISP. These subsets can both be thought of as logic programming languages, but the logic of pure LISP is restricted to recursive function definitions, while that of PROLOG permits definitions of arbitrary relations. This is what gives rise to the use of backtracking control structure, multiple return values, and logical variables. Pure PROLOG, then, can be thought of as a conceptual extension of pure LISP.

The creators of LISP, however, recognised that "although this language (pure LISP) is universal in terms of computable functions of symbolic expressions, it is not convenient as a programming system without additional tools to increase its power". (McCarthy *et al*. 1962). What was added to LISP was a set of operations for directly manipulating the pointer structures that represent the abstract symbolic expressions forming the semantic domain of pure LISP. LISP thus operates at two distinct levels of abstraction; simple things can be done quite elegantly at the level of recursive functions of symbolic expressions, while more complex tasks can be dealt with at the level of operations on pointer structures. Both levels, though, are conceptually coherent and, in a sense, complete.

PROLOG also has extensions to its purely logical core that most users agree are essential to its use as practical programming language. These extensions, however, do not have the kind of uniform conceptual basis that the structure manipulation features of LISP do. Such features as the "cut" operation for terminating backtracking, "assert" and "retract" for altering the PROLOG database, and predicates that test whether variables are free or bound are all powerful and useful devices, but they do not share any common semantic domain of operation. There is nothing categorically objectionable about any of these features in isolation, but they do not fit together in a coherent way. The result is that, while PROLOG provides a very powerful set of tools, the effective use of those tools depends to a greater extent than with many other languages on the ingenuity of the programmer and his acquaintance with the lore of the user community. To be fair, this last statement is true of LISP as well, especially with regard to recent extensions, such as Flavors. But it seems that with PROLOG one is forced into this domain of semantic uncertainty sooner than with LISP.

This suggests that if PROLOG is really to replace LISP as the language of choice for AI systems, it should be given a more powerful and more conceptually coherent set of nonlogical extensions to the basic logic-programming paradigm, analogous to LISP's nonlogical extensions to the recursive-function paradigm. This suggestion would no doubt be resisted by purists who see the present nonlogical features of PROLOG as already departing too far from the semantic elegance of a system where the correctness of a program can be judged simply by whether all of its statements are true; but that is an idealised vision whose practical realization is doubtful.

One can make a plausible argument that the advent of massively parallel computer architectures will change this situation. For the type of problem that would normally be solved by an algorithm that changes data structures, using an imperative language typically requires fewer computation steps than using a declarative language but creates more timing dependencies. Thus parallel architectures and declarative languages are well matched, because the architecture provides the greater computational resources required by the language, and the language provides the lack of timing dependencies required to take advantage of the architecture. It remains to be seen, however, for how wide a class of problems the speedups due to parallelism outweigh the additional computation steps required.

PROLOG as an inference system. Whatever its merits purely as a programming language, much of the current enthusiasm for PRO-LOG undoubtedly stems from the impression that, because a PROLOG interpreter can be viewed as an automatic theorem-prover, PROLOG itself can be used as the reasoning module of an intelligent system. This is true to an extent, but only to a limited extent. The major limitation is that all practical logic programming systems to date, including PROLOG, are based, not on full first-order logic, but on the Horn-clause subset of first-order logic.

The easiest way to view Horn-clause logic is to say that axioms must be either atomic formulas such as ON(A,B) or implications whose consequent is an atomic formula and whose antecedent is either an atomic formula or a conjunction of atomic formulas:

$$(ON(x,y) \land ABOVE(y,z)) \supset ABOVE(x,z)$$

Furthermore, the only queries that can be posed are those that can be expressed as a disjunction of conjunctions of atomic formulas:

$$(ON(A,B) \land ON(B,C)) \lor (ON(C,B) \land ON(B,A))$$

These limitations mean that no negative formulas – e.g., $\neg ON(A,B)$ – can ever be asserted or inferred, and no disjunction can be inferred unless one of the disjuncts can be inferred. Thus, Horn-clause logic gives up two of the main features of first-order logic that permit reasoning with incomplete knowledge: being able to say or infer that one of two statements is true without knowing which is true, and being able to distinguish between knowing that a statement is false and not knowing that it is true.

The question of quantification is more complicated. Horn-clause logic does not permit quantifiers *per se*, but it does allow formulas to contain function symbols and free variables, and there is a result (Skolem's theorem) to the effect that, with these devices, any quantified formula can be replaced by one without quantifiers.

However, this quantifier-elimination theorem does not apply to most logic programming systems, because of the way they implement unification (pattern matching).

According to the usual mathematical definition of unification, a variable cannot be unified with any expression in which it is a proper subexpression. That is, x will not unify with $F(G(x))$, because there is no fully instantiated value for x that will make these two expressions identical. The test for this condition is usually called "the occur check". The occur check is computationally expensive, though, so most logic programming systems omit it for the sake of efficiency. There is a mathematically rigorous foundation for unification operation without the occur check, based on infinite trees, but this version of unification is *not* compatible with the quantifier-elimination techniques usually used in automatic theorem-proving. In particular, without the occur check, a logic programming system cannot properly distinguish between formulas that differ only in quantifier scope, such as, $\forall x(\exists y(P(x,y)))$ and $\exists y(\forall x(P(x,y)))$. That is, the system cannot distinguish between the statement that every person has a mother, and the statement that every person has the same mother.

These restrictions are so severe that PROLOG is almost never used as a reasoning system without using the extra-logical features of the language to augment its expressive power. In particular, the usual practice is to define negation in the system, using the "cut" operation, so that ⌐P can be inferred by having an attempt to infer P terminate in failure. Making this extension permits the implementation of nontrivial reasoning systems in PROLOG in a very direct way, but it amounts to making "the closed-world assumption": any statement that cannot be inferred to be true is assumed to be false. To adopt this principle, though, is to give up entirely on trying to reason with incomplete knowledge, which is the main advantage that logic-based systems have over their rivals.

To see what one gives up in making the closed-world assumption, consider the following problem, adapted from Moore (1980). Three blocks, A, B, and C, are arranged as shown in Figure 3.1.

A is green, C is blue, and the color of B is unstated. In this arrangement of blocks, is there a green block next to a block that is not green? It should be clear with no more than a moment's reflection that the answer is "yes". If B is green, it is a green block next to the nongreen block C; if B is not green then A is a green block next to the nongreen block B.

To solve this problem, a reasoning system must be able to withold judgment on whether block B is green; it must know that either B is green or B is not green without knowing which; and it must use this fact to infer that *some* blocks stand in a certain relation to each other, without being able to infer which blocks these are. None of this is possible in a system that makes the closed-world assumption.

This is not to say that using PROLOG as a reasoning system with the closed-world assumption is always a bad thing to do. For applications where the closed-world assumption is justified, using PROLOG in this way can be extremely efficient – possibly more efficient than anything that can be programmed in LISP (for much the same reasons that top-down parsing is so efficient in PROLOG). But not all situations justify the closed-world assumption, and where it is not justified, the fact that PROLOG can be viewed as a theorem-prover is irrelevant. The usefulness of PROLOG in such a case will depend only on its utility as a programming language for implementing other inference systems.

3.5   Conclusions

In this paper we have reviewed three possible applications of formal logic in artificial intelligence: as a tool for analyzing knowledge-representation formalisms, as a source of representation formalisms and reasoning methods, and as a programming language. As an analytical tool, the mathematical framework developed in the study of formal logics is simply the only tool we have for analyzing anything as a representation. There is little more to say, other than to note all the efforts to devise representation formalisms that have come to grief for lack of adequate logical analysis.

The other two applications are more controversial. A large segment of the AI community believes that any representation or deduction system based on standard logic will necessarily be too inefficient to be of any practical value. We have argued that such negative conclusions are based on experiments in which there was insufficient control of the deductive process, and we have presented a number of cases in which better control would lead to more efficient

Figure 3.1: In the blocks world

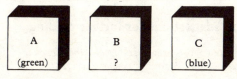

processing. Moreover, we have argued that when an application involves incomplete knowledge of the problem, only systems based on logic seem adequate to the task.

The use of logic as a basis for programming languages is the most recent application of logic within AI. We had two major points to make in this area. First, current logic programming languages (i.e., PROLOG) need to be more developed in their *non*logical features before they can really replace LISP as the primary language for developing intelligent systems. Second, as they currently exist, logic programming languages are suitable for direct use as inference systems only in a very restricted class of applications.

After thirty years, where does the use of logic in AI now stand? In all fairness, one would have to say that its promise has yet to be proven – but, of course, that is true for most of the field of AI. It may be that, if the promise of logic is to be fulfilled, it will have to come in a remerging of two of the main themes explored in this paper: automatic deduction and logic programming. Logic programming grew out of the realization that, if automated reasoning systems are to perform efficiently, the information they are given must be carefully structured in much the same way that efficient computer programs are structured. But, instead of using that insight to produce more efficient reasoning systems, the developers of logic programming applied their ideas to more conventional programming problems. Perhaps the time is now right to take what has been learned about the efficient use of logic in logic programming, and apply it to the more general use of logic in automated reasoning. This just might produce the kind of basic technology for reasoning systems on which the development of the entire field depends.

Acknowledgements

Preparation of this paper was made possible by a gift from the System Development Foundation as part of a coordinated research effort with the Center for the Study of Language and Information, Stanford University.

This paper has also appeared as "The role of Logic in Artificial Intelligence", Artificial Intelligence Center Technical Note 335, SRI International, Menlo Park, California (July 1984).

References and suggestions for further reading

Colmerauer, A. (1978). Metamorphosis grammars. In *Natural-Language Communication with Computers*, ed. L. Bolc. Berlin: Springer-Verlag.

Hayes, P.J. (1973). Computation and deduction. In *Proc. 2nd Symposium on Foundations of Computer Science*, Czechoslovak Academy of Sciences, pp. 105–116. September 1973.

Hayes, P.J. (1977). In defence of logic. In *Proc. Fifth International Joint Conference on Artificial Intelligence*, Cambridge, Massachusetts, pp. 559–565. 22–25 August 1977.

Kintch, N. (1974). *The Representation of Meaning in Memory*. New Jersey: Lawrence Erlbaum.

Kowalski, R.A. (1974). Predicate logic as a programming language. In *Information Processing 74*, pp. 569–574. Amsterdam: North-Holland.

Kowalski, R.A. (1979). *Logic for Problem Solving*. New York: Elsevier North-Holland.

McCarthy, J. *et al.* (1962). *LISP 1.5 Programmer's Manual*. Cambridge, Mass.: MIT Press.

Moore, R.C. (1980). *Reasoning from Incomplete Knowledge in a Procedural Deduction System*. New York: Garland.

Newell, A. (1980). The knowledge level. Presidential Address, American Association for Artificial Intelligence, AAAI80, Stanford University, Stanford, California. 19 August 1980. *AI Magazine*, Vol. 2, No. 2, pp. 1-20. Summer 1981.

Robinson, J.A. (1965). A machine-oriented logic based on the resolution principle. *Journal of the Association for Computing Machinery*, Vol. 12, No. 1, pp. 23-41. January 1965.

Warren, D.H.D., Pereira, L. M. & Pereira, F.C.N. (1977). PROLOG – the language and its implementation compared with LISP. In *Proc. Symposium on Artificial Intelligence and Programming Languages* (ACM); SIGPLAN Notices, Vol. 12, No. 8; and *SIGART Newsletter*, No. 64, pp. 109–115. August 1977.

Woods, W.A. (1975). What's in a Link: Foundations for Semantic Networks. In *Representation and Understanding*, ed. D.G. Bobrow and A. Collins, pp. 35–82. New York: Academic Press.

4 Natural language processing

STANLEY ROSENSCHEIN

4.1 Introduction

Although this essay is entitled "Natural language processing", a large part of it will be devoted to examining the various roles that logic can play in AI applications generally by looking at natural language as an interesting case study. The paper is thus divided into two parts, the first consisting of an overview of some of the main issues in natural language processing (NLP) and the second containing and analysis of the roles played by logic.

Why study natural language?. The goal of research in natural language processing is to develop machines that can understand and generate human language so that humans might interact with them in much the same way they interact with other humans. There are several reasons why this an important goal. The first is simply the obvious practical utility of having machines use ordinary language; as computers proliferate, any development that would render them more usable by the average man is to be welcomed. Research in NLP is also important as an accelerator for work in Artificial Intelligence (AI) generally, especially in the areas of knowledge representation, inference, and planning. Perhaps the main reason for studying natural language processing, however, has to do with its scientific importance and the light it promises to shed on the fundamental nature of thought and communication.

On the practical side, there are two technological developments which would make the wide-spread appearance of natural language processing almost inevitable. The first is already upon us, and that is small, fast, inexpensive processors and memory of increased capacity which are becoming available and which will make it feasible to provide language-processing as a module in systems designed primarily to do something else without placing undue strain on the system's resources (or the customer's pocketbook). The second development, unfortunately, does not appear to be as imminent as the first, and that is continuous speech recognition. One of the largest obstacles to the widespread use of even those natural language techniques that already exist is simply the fact that in most systems the input has to be typed. If speech recognition technology were available, there would be far greater motivation for actually building systems with extensive natural language abilities.

The need for natural language interaction with machines can be better appreciated by considering the increasing behavioural complexity of devices we encounter in our daily lives. Even today many devices are becoming somewhat complex and capable in their behaviours. It suffices to think of microwave ovens or pre-programmable videocassette recorders. The primary mode of communication with these devices right now is by pushing buttons, lots of little buttons. If you have ever tried to program your videocassette recorder by pushing these little buttons you will know how difficult a task that can actually be – despite all the effort that goes into "human-engineering" them.

Imagine a world of the future in which everyday devices were far more complex and capable than these. Every device in one's environment would have built into it very powerful computers with large amounts of memory and great processing power. In such a world, each device would be capable of a range of behaviours much broader and more subtle than those exhibited by the devices of today. In such a world, one would like to be able to control these devices without laboriously indicating every micro-action the device is to perform. Instead, one would like simply to communicate one's intentions or desires to the device or to convey arbitrary auxiliary information that will help the device decide what to do in order that those desires might be met. This is precisely where natural language excels; it offers a brief, natural, and cognitively efficient way to carry out communication of this sort.

Areas of activity in natural language research. The analysis of natural language systems is ordinarily broken into levels. At the bottom are the acoustic, phonological, and morphological levels, which for present purposes can be though of collectively as the word-extraction level. Next there is the syntactic level, which has to do with the well-formedness of utterances and the description of syntactic structure, for example, through the use of phrase markers. Then there is the semantic level which has to do with the meaning or content of the utterance, and finally there is the pragmatic level which has to do with the role of the utterance in advancing the speaker's purposes in the broader discourse context.

These levels each have dual aspects depending on whether one is concerned with understanding or with generation of natural language. Although it is widely agreed that the levels need not correspond directly to "phases" of processing in any interesting sense, still it is often convenient to describe natural language systems as if they did. Thus, one can postulate distinct data-structure representations for each level and view the program as embodying mappings from representations at one level to representations at another. For instance, on the understanding side we imagine the program "climbing" the levels by constructing parse trees, meaning representations, and finally representations of the speaker's beliefs and intentions. On the generation side, the program performs synthesis operations that map the representation of an intention to perform some communicative act to a structure that fixes the propositional content of the utterance and then to a syntactic structure and ultimately to commands that perform the actual output.

Keeping this division into levels in mind, we will now evaluate the status of each area and its associated technology.

Speech. In the area of speech recognition the ultimate goal is to have a machine understand unrestricted continuous speech. The successes to date have been limited. Discrete speech is a much easier problem and there are commercially available systems that do manage discrete speech recognition with severely limited vocabularies and number of speakers. Continuous speech can only be recognised under even more special conditions. The problem is simply combinatorial explosion. We do not yet know how to apply the constraints that are required to pick one interpretation from all the interpretations that are potentially compatible with the raw speech signal.

Syntax. Syntax, on the other hand, has been one of the most successful areas. In applications where word extraction is non-problematic (e.g. because of typed input) and where only syntactic parse trees are required, the technology is really quite good. There are several efficient parsing techniques that seem to work well for natural languages. In the area of grammars, among the successful very large grammmars are the DIAGRAM grammar developed by Jane Robinson at SRI (Robinson, 1982) and the Linguistic String Project grammar developed by Naomi Sager at NYU (Sager, 1981). These grammars have been developed over a period of many years and each covers substantial portions of English. It should be noted that while the greatest amount of research has been done on English, there now appear to be similar efforts under way for other languages, including Japanese.

The research goals in the area of syntactic processing include finding even more efficient algorithms for parsing large, linguistically accurate, computer-based grammars expressed in compact grammatical and meta-grammatical formalisms. Some of the problems remaining include the handling of errorful or anomalous inputs and false starts (which, of course, are very frequent in real discourse) and the smooth integration of syntactic processing with other kinds of processing.

Semantics. In the area of semantics the goals include the construction of general systems for meaning representation, often based on some variety of logical form, in which the content of sentences might be expressed and manipulated by the computer. Researchers are also interested in the analysis of specific semantic phenomena. Mathematical theories of meaning developed in the tradition of formal philosophy and theoretical linguistic semantics have provided much of the inspiration in computational semantics of natural language. However, the need for computational manipulation of meaning representations adds a new dimension to semantic issues. Furthermore, there are numerous interesting questions having to do with the relationship of the mathematical models of meaning to syntax-directed transduction methods for expressing computationally-oriented semantics in the grammar and for recovering logical forms during the parsing.

There have been a number of partial successes in semantics, including several applications of techniques inspired by Montague's model-theoretic semantics to natural language processing, and more recently Barwise and Perry's Situation Semantics (Barwise and Perry, 1983). Enormous problems remain, however. First, there are a very large number of problematic semantic domains: e.g. mass terms, actions, tense, aspect. There is a huge linguistic and philosophical literature on the semantics of particular constructions (and even particular words) and still no general agreement on the best semantic analysis of a great many frequently-occurring constructions. Another problem has to do with the way that approaches developed for the semantics of language dovetail with general reasoning and representation techniques. Any program that is to be able to reason from the content of a sentence to some facts about the world requires that the gap between meaning representation and knowledge representation be bridged.

Pragmatics. Finally, in the area of pragmatics the goal is to develop systems that that can understand multi-sentence texts or extended discourse, handling problems of reference resolution in context, managing discourse state over time, and inferring the intentional state of the speaker from the utterances spoken in context. Successes in computational pragmatics are even more limited than in the case of semantics, but there are some beginnings. For instance, there are some computationally-oriented theories of focus and reference (e.g. Grosz, 1977, Sidner, 1978) and speech acts (e.g., Perrault and Cohen, 1980). There have also been some experimental programs that synthesise utterances by reasoning about the effects of the utterance on the state of mind of the hearer (Appelt, 1982).

Some of the problems that remain include integrating linguistic pragmatics into a general theory of action, describing the mechanisms of syntactically cued discourse structure, and developing a plausible model of belief and intention updating. Broadly viewed, pragmatics includes the application of general knowledge and reasoning to linguistic situations and as such presents problems that are extremely difficult, since they encompass many of the most challenging core research problems of AI.

4.2   The roles of logic in natural language processing

Having sketched these main areas of interest in natural language processing we now turn to the question of the roles played by logic in natural language processing. In trying to get from utterances actually spoken to information conveyed by those utterances, one might imagine taking several different routes. We shall argue that logic plays characteristically different roles on each of these routes but that each of these routes is promising and needs to be investigated as a strategy for achieving the goals of language processing. The routes have certain superficial similarities, so we will need to be very subtle in distinguishing the specific role played by logic in each of these strategies. The first two routes use logic as an internal representation language that the program manipulates in some fashion, while the third route uses logic only at the design level and doesn't view the program as manipulating logical expressions at all. The "representational" routes are further sub-classified according to whether logic is used as just a meaning representation language or as a more general notation for arbitrary reasoning about the world.

Route 1 – meaning as logical form. Let us take these routes one by one. Route 1 can be described as taking the viewpoint of "meaning as logical form". It is based on the metaphor that utterances are like expressions in a formal language. As the logicians have taught us, expressions in formal languages can be assigned model-theoretic interpretations. The tradition of viewing natural languages (e.g. English) as formal languages was started by Montague about a decade and a half ago and its popularity in the linguistic community has engendered numerous attempts to translate some of the results achieved in linguistics into the computational domain as well.

Taking the "meaning as logical form" metaphor as a starting point, the strategy for building a system for understanding English would be as follows. First, translate surface utterances of English into formulas in some artificial logical language that express (under the intended interpretation) the same content as the original English sentences. Next, have the computer formally manipulate these translations in a way that is faithful to their intended interpretations, for example by employing sound deductive techniques. This strategy actually forms the basis of many existing natural language systems.

The translation phase of the strategy is typically achieved by first recovering syntactic structure by building parse trees using a parser and a grammar in much the same way as a compiler would for parsing artificial languages like programming languages. The meaning representation is recovered by using syntax-directed transduction to build the logical form, that is, some internal data structure that represents the content of the sentence. Having recovered the logical form, inferences can then be performed, for example, by axiomatising the intended interpretation in some standard logic like first-order logic or in some specialised logic and then using theorem-proving techniques or other automated inference techniques to manipulate the formulas.

The passage from raw utterances to semantic meanings can be formalised by postulating several intermediate domains and relations between them. For instance, if we assume four domains of interest: utterance expressions, structural descriptions, logical form expressions, and models, we can view these as being related in turn by syntactic analysis (relating utterance expressions to structural descriptions), a translation relation (relating structural descriptions to logical forms), and an interpretation relation (relating logical forms to their model-theoretic meanings). The composition of these relations, of course, takes sentences to their truth-conditional meanings.

These relations are typically specified in detail by formal devices

Figure 4.1: Relating an utterance to its meaning

S → NP VP	VP′(NP′)
NP → John	j
NP → Mary	m
VP → V NP	$\lambda x.\ V'(x, NP')$
V → saw	$\lambda y.\lambda x.\ \text{Past(See }(x, y))$

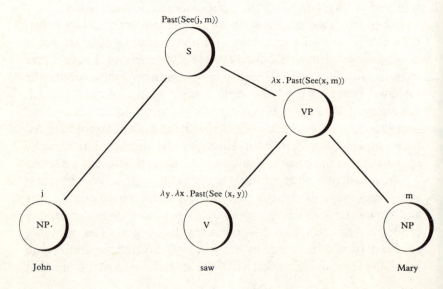

of the appropriate sort. For instance, the syntax and trans-lation relations are ordinarily given by a grammar, which may be in the form of phrase-structure rules, specifying how the constit-uents of a sentence are formed from sub-constituents, together with corresponding semantic rules, specifying how to build up the meanings of the constituent from the meanings of its parts. For example the simple grammar illustrated in Figure 4.1 might associate with the sentence "John saw Mary" the phrase marker (S (NP John)(VP (V saw)(NP Mary))), where S indicates "sentence", NP "noun phrase", VP "verb phrase", and V "verb". If the semantic rules are taken to be transduction rules, their application would produce a formula which is intended to be a representation of the content of the sentence: Past(See(j,m)).

The grammar with rule-by-rule transduction schemata takes the raw string "John saw Mary" to a parse tree and then to a logical form. At this point the computational linguist and the theoretical linguist part ways. The theoretical linguist (in the Montague tradition, at least) is primarily interested in the assignment of truth conditions to the sentence. He does this in an abstract mathematical way by defining a class of models and a satisfaction relation like $\vDash$ that holds (or fails to hold) between a model and a formula. For the compu-tational linguist, on the other hand, something more is required; simply knowing the truth conditions of the utterance is not sufficient. He would typically define a new relation, which might be notated $\Vdash$ (computable entailment), meaning that one expression is a deducible consequence of some (finite number of) other expressions. This relation should respect the abstract satisfaction relation but is not identical with it because this deducibility relation is intended to be computable. In fact, for most applications it should be efficiently computable.

If the relations of syntactic analysis, semantic transduction and computable entailment are implementated in the form of computer programs, we have the building blocks of at least a rudimentary language understanding system. For instance, one could build a simple automated question-answering system, that behaves as illustrated in Figure 4.2.

After typing in the sentence "John saw Mary", the user can query the system as to whether John saw anyone. The system responds "yes" because it can relate each utterance to its logical form by applying the computer procedures implementing the syntactic analysis and translation relations. Finally, by applying its computable entailment relation it can deduce that the propositional content of the query is a consequence of the first sentence and so the answer should be "yes". Although this dialogue is quite trivial, it illustrates how deduction and translation figure together in a system based on logical forms.

There are some important problems that have been glossed over in this example. For example, why did the system decide to treat the second sentence as a sincere query and answer "yes"? The sentence could have been a rhetorical question. In fact, in a real conversation it would be odd for someone to ask for information which he had just volunteered in the previous utterance (barring temporary lapses of memory, etc.). So in some sense the simple question-answering system built along these lines already has hard-wired into it some crude mechanisms for the recognition of speech act types. A second point which has been glossed over has to do with the need for additional axioms or "meaning postulates". For example, there would have to be some axioms about the Past operator that express facts about temporal relationships.

Several points should be noticed about the "meaning as logical form" approach as a whole. First, the meanings of symbols in the logical-form language need to be stipulated by the system designer. While this may seem unavoidable, it will be called into question later. Second, the translation relation takes referring expressions onto terms of fixed denotations at translation time. In other words, at the time at which the program does translations it has to determine quite a bit about the meaning of the sentence, and sometimes it does so in a context where that information is not yet available. For instance, in our example of "John saw Mary", the word "Mary" in English does not really pick out any given individual in the world; "Mary" is just a name and there may be many people named "Mary". Yet the translation procedure seems to require that some particular constant (e.g. m_1 or m_2) be assigned at translation time.

Figure 4.2: A simple automated question and answer session

User:	John saw Mary.	[Past(See(j,m))]
System:	OK.	[recorded in knowledge base]
User:	Did John see someone?	[Past(∃x.See(j,x))]
System:	Yes.	[because
		Past(See(j,m)) ⊩ Past(∃x.See(j,x))]

Many methods have been employed to finesse this particular problem, but none are entirely satisfactory. In any event, the issue of premature binding to constants is pervasive in the logical-form approach; the entire approach is founded on producing a logical form that expresses the full content of the sentence immediately upon syntactic analysis. Clearly, this is not always possible. It would be desirable to have a logical form which allows for the expression of partial information about the interpretation of the sentence. For example, consider the sentence "the man's dog did it". What would be the logical form of such a sentence? As stated, there is almost no information in the sentence! The best that one could do would perhaps be something like

Past(P(d)) & Dog(d) & Man(m) & R(m,d) which can be paraphrased as "In the past some property P held of d, and d is a dog, and m is a man, and some relation R holds between m and d." What is the interpretational status of P and R? In some sense they can be viewed as uninterpreted relation parameters, but formulas of this sort pose numerous inference problems.

In addition to this problem, the logical-form approach has problems in dealing with general anaphora, speech acts, vagueness of intended interpretation, and incomplete sentences (because we can't assign a full logical form to an incomplete sentence). Also, in general the system needs to understand sentences that it ought not necessarily to believe. Thus it needs to have some way of distinguishing expressions that designate the content of the sentence from the expressions that designate its own beliefs about the world. At this point one is tempted to despair of the attempt to use of logic in natural language processing and cry "Help!"

Route 2 – knowledge as logical theory. All is not lost, however. Logic can still be used, although in a quite different way, to address many of these problems. What really appears to be necessary is for the speaker and the hearer to reason about the structure and content of the communication event, i.e. the utterance in context. This does not have to be carried out by employing the strategy of translating from a single utterance into a single logical form. Since logic is a way of formally representing general reasoning that a language user might perform, it seems natural to view the language user as manipulating logical assertions about his world at large and the particular part of his world which is the linguistic communication event in question.

This point of view leads to the Route 2 approach, i.e. "knowledge as logical theory". In this approach logic is used as a representation language for beliefs in general. The strategy associated with Route 2 is based on the following perspective. Utterances are like other real events in the world, and the interpretation of utterances is like the interpretation of other perceptual stimuli. Seeing objects on a table and hearing someone say something about those objects are both perceptual stimuli of a fundamentally similar nature, and both have to be reasoned about and interpreted. Furthermore, the generation of utterances is like the production of other purposeful actions. After all, what is the difference between moving one's tongue and moving one's arm? The effects of one might be more structured and more highly complex, but in some fundamental sense they are analogous.

A natural strategy, then, for building a language-understanding system would be to develop some general cognitive architecture, say along the lines of belief-desire-intention (BDI) psychology. Logical assertions can be employed as data structures to represent the content of a machine's cognitive state, i.e. these data structures somehow embody what the machine knows about the world. General techniques would be developed for updating mental state and for producing actions. Linguistic behaviours would be handled as a special case – a very important special case, no doubt, one with a great deal of rich structure and so on, but still very much a special case of the interpretation/action paradigm.

The first step in carrying out this strategy is to formalise belief-desire-intention psychology. A starting point would be to look at the ways in which mental states of agents are described in ordinary language. In ordinary language we use propositional attitude sentences to describe mental states; we say things like "x believes that p holds", or "x wants p to hold," or "x intends to do a." That is, we describe the internal state of individuals by putting the individuals into relations with propositions. A natural computational architecture based on this idea would view the computational state of the computer at any instant as consisting of three collections of data structures, encoding roughly the beliefs, desires, and intentions of the computer (viewed under this metaphoric interpretation.) In addition there would be some reasoning component that acts on these data structures. Among the reasoning processes would be inference processes that cause beliefs to be revised as new stimuli are processed and planning processes that transform desires together with beliefs about the consequences of one's actions into intentions which eventually yield actions.

Under this strategy, beliefs, desires, and intentions are operationalised as data structures, and reasoning and planning are realised as procedures that manipulate these data structures. Of course, not any set of data structures or procedures will do; they should behave in some well-defined fashion, satisfy certain important properties, or maintain certain invariant relations. The philosophical literature is filled with axiomatic formulations of relations that might obtain between (parts of) our mental state and mental processes. For example we might require certain relations between beliefs such as consistency, closure under deduction, accuracy of introspection, etc. One especially important relation might be called "rationality"; an agent is rational if it forms intentions to act in a way it believes will achieve its desires. Rationality is a three-place invariant relationship between beliefs, desires and intentions. The axiomatic formulations of these relationships between components of mental state could be used by a system designer as a formal specification, and one can imagine designing a system to maintain rationality or other similar relations as invariants.

So much for the general architecture of a cognitive system; how does this framework specialise to the linguistic case? Let us start with beliefs. Linguistic beliefs can be viewed as falling into two categories, the (relatively) fixed beliefs and the dynamic beliefs. Examples of fixed beliefs would be the rules of grammar, which can be thought of as beliefs about the linguistic competence of language-using agents in the world. Many language processing systems, especially those based on logic programming languages, e.g. definite clause grammars (DCGs), a PROLOG-like grammar formalism (Pereira and Warren, 1980), already use "declarative" representations of grammatical knowledge and thus can be viewed as containing assertional beliefs about grammar. Taken to the limit, this assertional approach would make no essential distinction between knowledge that happens to be about grammatical structures and knowledge that is about cups and saucers.

Besides the fixed beliefs there are dynamic beliefs, such as linguistic beliefs that change rapidly throughout the discourse, for example beliefs about utterances, their parse trees, their meanings, the discourse situation, and so on. The key here is that each of these beliefs might be represented in a rather atomic fashion rather than being represented collectively in a single parse tree and logical form as in Route 1. With respect to desires, a typical desire of linguistic import might be the desire to change someone else's state of mind, the desire to cause someone else to believe something, or to cause them to act in a certain way. Similar remarks hold for intentions of linguistic import.

What role can logic play as a representation language for these linguistic mental entities? Looking first at syntax, it seems that logic might have little to contribute since syntax is concerned with the assignment of parse trees to sentences, a straightforward problem for which there are well-known representations and algorithms. It is surprising, therefore, that some computational linguists have begun to propose the use of assertions to represent syntactic structures for internal linguistic reasons, for reasons having nothing to do with the goal of incorporating linguistic processing into a general cognitive framework. For example Mitch Marcus (Marcus *et al*, 1983) proposed that rather than constructing parse trees that encode everything there is to know about some piece of syntactic structure, we incrementally develop a set of assertions as linguistic processing proceeds. These assertions simply express certain domination relations obtaining between nodes in some hypothetical parse tree which may never actually be explicitly constructed.

For instance, Figure 4.3 shows an explicit parse tree contrasted with a description of a parse tree represented as a collection of formulas asserting that node n_1 dominates node n_2, node n_1 dominates node n_3, and so on. In principle, these assertions could even contain disjunctions to represent a state of even greater uncertainty. Using assertions allows us to have partiality of description in a way that explicit parse trees do not. This feature of partiality would be relevant, for instance, in trying to describe what a system knows in midstream while processing an utterance or giving the system the ability to recover some information in situations where it only heard the second half of a sentence (which human language users frequently manage to do). It is desirable to have the system be able to draw at least some inferences in these situations and using logic to represent a state of partial knowledge in smaller, more atomic units would constitute one approach to this problem.

This idea can be extended from the domain of syntax to the domain of semantics as well. That is, one can describe the denotation of an utterance in a logical framework rather than actually exhibiting a full-blown logical form. Figure 4.4 illustrates for meaning representations the same kind of contrast between the explicit and the descriptive that we saw previously in the syntactic domain.

Where the logical form approach of route 1 requires that the sentence "John saw Mary" be translated all at once into the rather rigid form PAST(See(j,m)), the current descriptive approach allows the system to defer decisions where its information is lacking. For instance, by having a term denoting the referent of "John", certain further conclusions can be drawn even in the absence of the information of the form referent("John",...) = j_{33}. This is the main advantage of having a collection of rather smallish assertions about pieces of the utterance; further constraints are accumulated as more information is gathered. For instance, the system may discover fourteen sentences later that the denotation of the third sub-utterance (i.e., the referent of "John") turned out to be someone else or perhaps someone who hadn't been mentioned previously in the conversation. Having these rather smallish units gives the semantic component of the system the flexibility to make the most of the information it has at each point in time.

Just as the route 1 approach had its problems, there are several salient things to be noticed about this syntactified belief–desire–intention model used in route 2. One is the use of time variables. When one actually tries to carry out the route 2 strategy and build a system of this sort, the handling of time in the logical theory turns out to be crucial. After all, although the designer may have in mind a

Figure 4.3: Representations of a parse treee

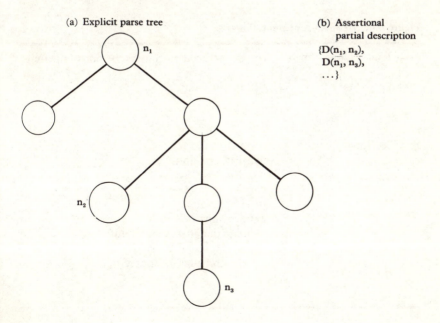

(a) Explicit parse tree

n_1

n_2

n_3

(b) Assertional
partial description
{$D(n_1, n_2)$,
$D(n_1, n_3)$,
...}

logical theory which talks about time, the system is embedded in time. There has to be some way for the system to manage its references to all the times it actually passes through. This is a rather technical point that goes beyond the scope of this paper; it has to do with how the system might reason about its experiences and actions over time and what kind of internal languages are appropriate for such reasoning.

An even greater challenge to the practicality of the route 2 strategy for actual system-building – though by no means an insuperable challenge – are the enormous practical difficulties involved in having a computational system deduce enough formulas to even approximate the degree of deductive closure ordinarily ascribed to human systems of belief. There is a fundamental but poorly understood trade-off between expressiveness of the logic used for describing a domain and the computational tractability of the associated deduction problem for that logic. This becomes quite a crucial point when dealing with theories that have as much structure and complexity as theories of syntactic, semantic, and pragmatic competence. To state the point another way, in using collections of assertional formulas to represent belief states closed under any reasonable approximation of logical entailment, it seems one is committed to some form of deductive processing. If beliefs are syntactified they have to be made

Figure 4.4: Meaning representations

(a) Explicit logical form	(b) Assertional partial description of meaning
"John saw Mary"	"John saw Mary"
↓	↓

Past(See(j,m))	u = [u1,u2,u3],
	word(u1) = "John",
	word(u2) = "saw",
	word(u3) = "Mary",
	utter(spkr,u,t),
	believe(spkr,t,
	    holds(denot(u2),⟨referent(u1,spkr,t),
	        referent(u3,spkr,t)⟩,
	        reftime(u2,spkr,t))),

...

explicit if they are to control the system's behaviour. The way to make implicit facts explicit is by deduction, and deduction is a very hard problem.

There is another problem with the route 2 approach, which, like the deduction problem, seems unavoidable. This problem has to do with arbitrariness of the interpretation of belief states. In the model we have described, belief states are regarded as collections of interpreted assertions, where the interpretations are those assigned, or stipulated, by the system designer. This is a somewhat unsettling state of affairs; it appears that the designer can change what the system knows without changing one comma in his program by merely deciding to regard the denotation of certain terms differently. For instance he may use the LISP S-expression (HAPPY JOHN) to mean that John is happy and build his entire system around that. If at some later time he decides that (HAPPY JOHN) doesn't mean that John is happy at all, but rather that Sam is sad, in one instant he has changed the knowledge that his system had. The sensitivity to the designer's choice of encoding is appropriate, say, for combinatorial algorithms, but it is quite unsatisfactory for a theory of knowledge; ideally we would like the system's knowledge to be independent of the whims of his designer.

Both the problem of deductive tractability and the arbitrariness of interpretation seem to be intrinsic to an over-literal operationalisation of folk psychology. What seems over-literal is the notion that every belief ascribed to an individual, whether it is a belief with linguistic content or a general belief about the world, needs to find its expression in the computer system as a corresponding data object. This is a rather rigid idea and, as we shall attempt to show, an unnecessary one. At first glance, however, there do not seem to be any alternatives to this approach. What other way could one imagine for getting a machine's behaviour to be effectively controlled by an implicit belief without first making that belief explicit as an expression or data object? Here again, we might be tempted to doubt the utility of logic and cry "Help!"

Route 3 – information as logical attunement. Here again, logic to the rescue. Recall that route 1 used logic as the target language for a translation process that produced rather rigid logical forms from surface utterances. Then we argued that to handle pragmatic phenomena effectively, the system had to reason about the world in general, including the linguistic part of the world, and we operationalised this reasoning as automated syntactic inference, with some suitable logic serving as the "language of thought". Now, we shall move one step further and argue that what is really required is for the designer of an intelligent system to reason in some metalanguage about the machine's states and their objective relationship to the states of the world in which the machine is embedded. This approach is closer in spirit to work on program specification and verification and has the advantage of decoupling the quantity of information that the machine possesses about the world from the structural complexity of the machine's states.

The route 3 approach to building complex behavioural systems, such as natural language systems, is based on a theory of information as logical attunement. Here the metaphor goes as follows. Utterances are like other physical events, their origins are in the mechanistic state transitions of physical systems. They are just part of the causal order of things which we model in some logical theory. The strategy for building a system in tune with its enviroment, especially with those parts of its enviroment exhibiting linguistic structure, is to develop a sound theoretical approach for relating states of machines to states of the enviroment. In such a theory logical assertions will be used in the metalanguage to characterise the information content of these various states, but the states themselves may or may not themselves encode logical assertions. Finally, develop synthesis techniques to transform the desired informational relationships into concrete machine designs, again handling linguistic behaviour as an important special case.

The basic idea of the route 3 approach is to develop a logic of situated automata, that is, automata whose inputs and outputs are interpreted as events in some world in which the automaton is embedded. This logic would be a "temporal" logic in the sense that it would allow us to reason about changes in conditions of the world over time. We will now briefly sketch some of the mathematical concepts that would lie at the heart of a theory of situated automata.

Let P denote the set (actually a lattice) of instantaneous world conditions, and let V denote the set of input stimuli of the automaton. If p is a condition, and v a stimulus, p/v will represent the strongest post-condition obtaining in the world given that event v has just occured and that p obtained just prior to v's occurence. The strongest post-condition operation is extended to sequences in the obvious way: $p/() = p$, $p/(v_1,...,v_n) = (p/v_1)/(v_2,...,v_n)$. Let p_0 denote a distinguished condition corresponding to the strongest condition that must obtain when the automaton is in its initial state (i.e., when the machine is turned on).

Given these basic concepts, one can define a set of world conditions that might be called the "knowable conditions" – roughly, world conditions that any automaton over V could positively recognise. Let P' denote this set. Mathematically, P' is defined to be $\{p_o/v|v \in V^\star\}$, where $V^\star$ represents the Kleene closure of V (i.e., the set of all finite sequences of inputs.) In general, P' will be a strict subset of P; that is, there will be many conditions that could obtain that the automaton in principle could never know about. Note that this contrasts with the route 2 "knowledge as logical assertion" approach, since under that approach the automaton could be said to "know" the condition named by any interpreted formula in its knowledge base.

Finally, we observe that by taking for each state of the machine the equivalence classes of input strings that leave it in that state, we obtain a "collapsing" of the knowable conditions P' to those information states that the automaton can actually be in. In other words, we can define a concept of information by relating the state of the machine to states of the world and viewing the machine in a given state, s, as "knowing" p if for any sequence $(v_1,...,v_n)$ leaving the machine in state s, $p_0/(v_1,...,v_n)$ entails p. Notice that the formulas expressing these conditions are objects that the designer of the machine manipulates, not the machine itself; the designer of the machine reasons in some logic about what the machine knows. The machine states themselves may have no explicit syntactic encoding of that knowledge.

Let us look at the linguistic case again and see what such a theory would say about linguistic utterances. It would be beyond the scope of this paper to attempt to give a detailed account of even a small fragment of language. The complexity of linguistic structure makes the development of such an account a formidable project in its own right. Nonetheless, we can sketch broadly what such an account would have to explain. A machine (or a person for that matter) that is exposed to the utterance "John saw Mary" would be transformed over time from state s_1 to state s_2. Let p_1 denote the information content of the machine in state s_1. The syntactic, semantic, and pragmatic content of the linguistic theory should explain how if the string (john, saw, mary) moves an English-speaking automaton from s_1 to s_2, the objective information content of s_2 (i.e., the strongest post-condition of p_1 over the sequence (john, saw, mary), assuming no collapsing states) would have as a consequence in the logic a formula p_2 expressing, say, that someone named John saw someone named Mary, etc. We reiterate that the formula p_2 does not have to be specifically encoded in the state of the machine.

The situated automata view has certain advantages. Deductive closure comes for free, since all of the entailments are "computed" in the metalanguage, and one does not require an infinite amount of memory or an infinite amount of resources on the part of the machine. In some sense the finite state of the machine already includes all of the consequences that there could be about what it knows. So the deductive-closure axiom, which at first seemed like a mere idealisation, actually turns out to be a theorem. So where did the paradox of the intractability of deduction go? The key lies in the fact that not every logical condition definable in the metalanguage has equal status as a potential belief state. There are lots of beliefs states that a machine cannot get into (just as there are many functions no machine can compute). However in an important sense it has nothing to do with the fundamental resource limitations of the agent.

There are many interesting connections between the route 2 and route 3 approaches when it actually comes to describing particular computations that a language system would have to carry out in order to understand some piece of language. The dichotomy is not as great as it might at first appear, but again, a detailed discussion is beyond the scope of this paper.

4.3   Conclusions

This section summarises some of the advantages and disadvantages of each of these three approaches to the use of logic for natural language processing and attempts to indicate some of the trade-offs. In route 1, "meaning as logical form", the primary advantage is that it is based directly on methods that have been studied in depth by linguists and logicans. The model theory is well understood and there are many well-known "off-the-shelf" parsing and translation algorithms that can be employed. There are also grammars that have been written that fit very well with this approach to language. The disadvantages are that it uses total information; the system actually has to construct the whole parse tree. Also, it is limited to linguistic input events; there is no obvious way of combining other perceptual events such as seeing a cup on the table and hearing the words "get me that cup". In addition, it is somewhat clumsy for pragmatic and discourse phenomena.

Some of the advantages of route 2 are precisely the disadvantages of route 1. Route 2 can handle partial information, it is more general-purpose, and it handles linguistic and non-linguistic beliefs about the world with equal ease (in principle), as well as linguistic and non-linguistic inputs. It is also close to folk psychology and thus is intuitive; it is the way we like to think about one another, our own states of mind, and what causes our behaviour. It tries to build the "cognitive" architecture of a natural language system around our commonsense view of how humans actually generate and understand linguistic behaviour.

One of the disadvantages of route 2 is the arbitrariness of the denotation of this internal language of thought, that is the fact that a designer can change the knowledge of the system by changing his attitude towards what certain of the symbols denote. A second disadvantage is the need to make implicit beliefs explicit all the time, that is, to do deductions which in many cases turn out to be of rather high computational complexity. This is a severe practical problem which has to date limited the usefulness of this approach to the use of logic in natural language systems.

Route 3 shares the advantage of generality with route 2. This approach is closer to the fundamental computational nature of a machine embedded in an enviroment. Also, it eliminates the seeming paradox of implicit beliefs by decoupling the infinity of consequences of one's beliefs from the structural complexity of the states they are embodied in. Some of the disadvantages of this approach are the complexity of the synthesis problem and the fact that it is a very foundational approach and we do not yet have all the superstructure that we need for building complex systems based on that approach. More work is needed on how to build up these complex processes that can be analysed in this information-theoretic way.

Acknowledgement

This work was supported, in part, by a gift from the System Development Foundation.

References and suggestions for further reading

Appelt, D. Planning natural-language utterances to satisfy Multiple Goals. SRI AI Center Technical Note 259. SRI International, Menlo Park, CA, March 1982.

Barwise, J. & Perry J. *Situations and Attitudes*, MIT Press. Cambridge, Massachusetts, 1983.

Cohen, P. & Perrault, C.R. Elements of a plan-based theory of speech acts. *Cognitive Science*, Vol. 3, No. 3, 1979, pp. 177–212.

Grosz, B. The representation and use of focus in a system for understanding dialogs.

SRI AI Center Technical Note 150. SRI International, Menlo Park, CA, June 1977.

Marcus, M., Hindle, D. & Fleck, M. d-theory: talking about talking about trees. Proceedings, 21st Annual Meeting of the Association for Computational Linguistics. Massachusetts Institute of Technology, Cambridge, Massachusetts, 15-17 June, 1983.

Pereira, F.C.N. & Warren, D.H.D. definite clause grammars for language analysis – a survey of the formalism and a comparison with augmented transition networks. *Artificial Intelligence*, Vol. 13, 1980, pp. 231–278.

Robinson, J. DIAGRAM: a grammar for dialogues. *Communications of the ACM*, Vol. 25, No. 1, January 1982, pp. 27–47.

Sager, N. *Natural Language Information Processing*. Addison-Wesley Publishing Company, Reading, Massachusetts, 1981.

Sidner, C. The use of focus as a tool for disambiguation of definite noun phrases. In D. Waltz (Ed.) *Proceedings, Theoretical Issues in Natural Langage Processing – 2, pp. 86-95, Urbana, Illinois, July 1978.*

5
THOMAS GARVEY
Knowledge based systems

5.1 Introduction

We might usefully start off by considering the first paragraph from a blurb in *Computerworld*, entitled " AI-like package sends helicopter designers soaring". Now at least they had the graciousness to say "AI-like". They start by asking "can seven army pilots with no programming knowledge teach a computer to think like a military commander in less than two days?" Now obviously they meant this as a rhetorical question, leading to the answer of how one could, but I have to say that the answer is emphatically "NO!"

First of all, you might wonder whether seven army pilots even think like military commanders themselves, and whether they are the appropriate experts. The unfortunate thing is that this type of claim leads people to believe that somehow you can, by use of the right tools, enable novices to cram a tremendous amount of knowledge and information into a computer program, which is then accessible to the great unwashed. I think this is just ludicrous. What I would like to leave you with at the end of this essay is the idea that expert systems do have a place, they accomplish some interesting things, they use some interesting techniques. But, by no means are they the vehicle by which novices will be somehow encoding tremendous amounts of knowledge.

5.2   Expert system architecture and use

What we are trying to do in expert systems work is to represent and store in a computer the specialised knowledge that an expert has that enables him to solve problems in a relatively limited domain. In Figure 5.1, the outermost fuzzy area is to represent the total knowledge of the person from whom we are trying to capture expertise. This is, as you certainly must have gathered from the previous two chapters, very difficult to encode, and very difficult to reason within in any automatic sense. Yet it is essential for the way people typically think and solve problems. The domain knowledge, on the other hand, tends to be more specific, a little less fuzzy we hope, but still fuzzy and still uses some general techniques, which at this point I think are also beyond the ken of computers, although we are aiming towards them. In expert systems we are really trying to take a fairly crisp sub-set of that domain knowledge; typically we

Figure 5.1: **Relationships between areas of knowledge**

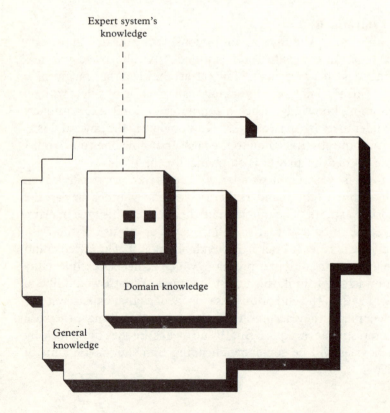

Expert system's
knowledge

Domain knowledge

General
knowledge

prefer not to overlap the edge of the fuzzy stuff. As long as the expert can specify things very crisply and delimit them and define them then in many cases we can make computer representations of them that are very useful. The main point is that the thing that makes people capable of doing the things they are doing and even experts expert, is the area in which all the *other* knowledge is embedded and we are very bad at handling that.

The structure of a typical expert system might look something like Figure 5.2. We have on one side the expert. By virtue of some knowledge acquisition system which is part of the state of the art but needs quite a lot of work, we capture and encode specific knowledge from him into a knowlege base typically represented by production rules or structures, taxonomies and things like that. This is then accessible to an inference system to draw conclusions based on inputs from a user. The user I/O system allows the person who is using the system, or in some cases the program that is using it, to enter information about situations or problems that he is interested in. The inference system takes advantage of the knowledge base to draw new conclusions and provide answers, results, advice, explanations and so forth back to the user.

The knowledge engineer (which by the way is another term which I really despise) is responsible for making this link between the knowlege base and the inference system. I have a problem with "knowledge engineers". I can understand what electrical engineering is; you have Maxwell's equations and that in some sense defines the whole branch of science. Mechanical engineers have Newton's laws and material equations. What do knowledge engineers have? Well they have production rules, and as we will see, it is a bit of a limited representation.

Be that as it may, there are many applications of knowledge based systems. We have seen applications in medical diagnosis such as MYCIN, one of the first real knowledge based systems (Shortliffe *et al.* 1979). We use these for diagnosis of virtually anything we can think of diagnosing. Faults in electrical circuits, mechanical equipment, people, that sort of thing. We use them to interpret the meanings of signals or the sources of signals. We have seen expert systems for assessing situations, particularly military situations. Probably the most effective, successful expert system is one called XCON, and its family of expert systems, used for designing and configuring computer systems (McDermott 1980). We are seeing

Figure 5.2: Components of an expert system

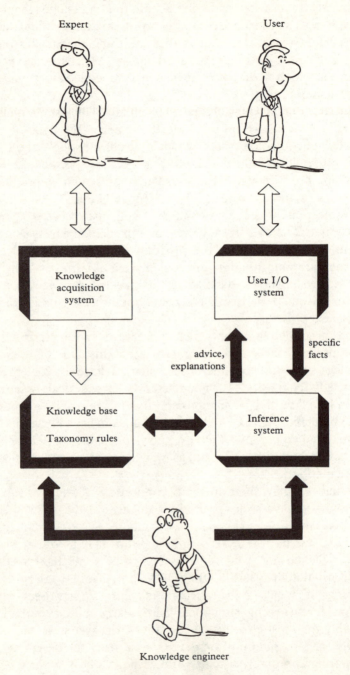

Knowledge engineer

more and more emphasis on the use of expert systems for making financial decisions. Should I really lend money to my brother-in-law? The military has started to use them for military intelligence.

Why do we really want to use expert systems?

Well if we could capture the expertise of some person who knows a lot about a certain domain we could get certain benefits. Typically they are good at what they do. Their performance is dependent more on the facts that you give them than on any particular computational procedure that is used to interpret those facts. Now I think that is probably a subject for argument, but at this point since our computational procedures are so limited, it probably is true that the facts are more important. We can develop the computational procedures incrementally. We can tune, refine and test them, do sensitivity analyses, and update them. Expert systems tend to have modular structures so you can change them relatively easily.

A caveat I have about the modifiability of expert systems is that you frequently cannot tell what is going to happen as a result of having changed it. There is no question about whether you can change it, and it is much easier to do than in a standard programming language.

Expert systems are frequently used in a consultation mode. That is, just as you sit down and you interact with an expert, you would like to do the same with an expert system. You would like to put in some information and get some results back. Look at the results, think about them for a little while, and put in other information, rather than just operating in batch mode (which would then be called pattern recognition). We would like to be able to use this sort of interactive approach, and most expert systems are set up to do that.

Typically expert systems provide some facility for making judgemental decisions. Although that is not universally true, there are a number of systems that are in some sense purely logic based, that use only Boolean statements. Most expert systems have to have some sort of explanation capability, or you won't really believe them. One of the real keys to a successful expert system is the ability to match the style of reasoning and the interests of the user, so the interface, and the verification, are extremely important.

Should we manage to capture an expert's information successfully, we get a number of benefits. In the system itself we get repeatable and precise conclusions. We can do "what if" scenarios, and get results back like a super Visicalc. We can, by sensitivity analyses, decide what factors are the pivotal factors in making decisions. Given that you have amortised the knowledge engineering phase, it is cheap to consult these things. They are available, given your computer system, 24 hours a day, and they are relatively immortal.

They are useful for education, because you can give students some problems and let them work with them with the system to guide them through and explain things to them. However, I think this may be true more often in theory than in practice. Another major benefit of expert systems is that they do provide an encoding method for experts in other domains that frequently leads to a better explanation of facts and procedures. In the geology domain, we found that geologists became very familiar with the production rule style of representation. They started writing down all their information in terms of production rules. There may soon be a new geology text which takes a very different approach to explaining fundamental models and processes in geology. Of course, having to think about what he has always taken for granted sometimes sharpens an expert's thinking on his own subject.

The geologists that we had at SRI were helping us to build the expert system called PROSPECTOR (Duda *et al.* 1979). I am going to use that as an example throughout this essay. It is old but most of the basic mechanisms and functions are still valid and useful today. They haven't been replaced by newer and better methods yet. It operates in real time (certainly in geological real time). Actually, for those of us who think that real time is hitting carriage return and seeing the answer come out, it even operates in that type of real time. It has upwards of 20 different models, where a model is a unified group of information about a particular type of ore deposit. PROSPECTOR's real forte was in representing models of hard rock mineral deposits; molybdenum, copper,zinc. Some of the models have upwards of 200 rules, and altogether they contain more than 500 rules, in all the different models.

It works, of course, better than the average geologist, like MYCIN worked better than the average GP, and I suppose as all the others work better than the average nonspecialist. It made a prediction of a new molybdenum deposit, which I have heard estimated as worth more than 100 million dollars to the company that found it. Actually the way I heard it estimated was, "it is worth more than 100 million dollars, which more than repays all the money that has been spent on AI to date". Of course it doesn't repay the people who spent the money on AI to date, but that must be next, obviously. It uses graphical input and output, which is very important. It also allows an English-like interface. It explains things to you in real English, because that was typed in by the designers. It also lets you type things in a sort of pseudo-English which for most of us is probably enough. A Knowledge Acquisition System called KAS was specifically built for PROSPECTOR.

Now, in the rest of this essay, I am going to very quickly go over things like what's in the knowledge base? What sorts of things do we want to encode? What does it mean to perform inferences over the knowledge base? How do users interact with a typical expert system? How do we apply our knowledge and encode it? And I will say something about the state of the art.

5.3   Knowledge classes

We start off by noting a little bit about the kind of knowledge we would like to incorporate in the system. We might think of knowledge as being expressed on a number of dimensions which in some sense are orthogonal to one another. We are interested in how knowledge is used. Some knowledge describes situations and other knowledge tells you what to do in certain situations. Some knowledge is very certain. Some knowledge is very uncertain. Some knowledge is very specific, and some knowledge is very general.

Of course any particular piece of knowledge will fall somewhere along any one of those dimensions. Look at how knowledge is used. We might say that the statement "Socrates is a man" is descriptive. A little more prescriptive statement is "To prove that X is mortal we might confirm that X is a man." It is telling us how to do something, or giving us some insight into what might be required to do something. Even more prescriptive might be a metarule that says "to analyse porphyry copper deposits use the PCBA model". Now that's a whole set of rules. In some sense a whole knowledge base unto itself. Its a statement that's really telling you at a metalevel how to use knowledge. We want to be able to encode all those types of knowledge.

Knowledge may be certain or uncertain. Some knowledge is provable. For example, "Socrates is human". In most expert systems we are unable to deal strictly with these Boolean types of statements. We are forced to probabilistic statements, "the likelihood that copper is present is .29" is a probabilistic statement. If we say "the identity of X is somewhere in the set (Tom, Dick, Harry and Georgette)" then we've made a statement about X but it's uncertain and yet we don't have any numbers that we can put on it. If we said "the likelihood that X is a fighter aircraft is between .62 and .83," in some sense we are constraining it. Now I might say that there is a certainty that Socrates is spinning in his grave, because he has been linked with fighter aircraft here, but that would probably remain to be validated.

Some knowledge is very specific, for example, "Socrates is a man." "All men are mortal" is a little less specific. It's saying something about a class. The statement "to prove h(x), prove $\neg$ h(x) is false," is very general. Once again we have a number of points along that spectrum. Typically, we would like to be able to encode all of these types in our knowledge base, but we are unable to do quite everything. We are very good at the specific. The general gets a little harder.

5.4   Knowledge representation

One way we represent the knowledge that we are using is by a thing called a production rule. That's about the most popular, well known, and most easily understood representation. Other representations that are useful are more structured representations. These allow inheritance of properties, multi-slot relations and more general structures for propagation of information such as dependency graphs.

A production rule looks sort of like this. It is an IF – THEN rule that says IF certain evidence is present THEN we can infer the hypothesis is true, usually with some sort of strength associated with it (which is how we get uncertainty into our rules). We can represent it graphically by a picture like Figure 5.3; evidence on one side and the hypothesis on the other.

Now of course, one man's hypothesis is another man's evidence. So we can chain these together to get networks of rules, where we want to propagate information throughout this network to reach some sort of consistent set of beliefs. Consistency turns out to be one of the difficulties.

Examples of rules are the following. In the XCON system for

Figure 5.3: Structure and notation for production rules

S

IF ⟨EVIDENCE⟩ THEN ⟨HYPOTHESIS⟩.

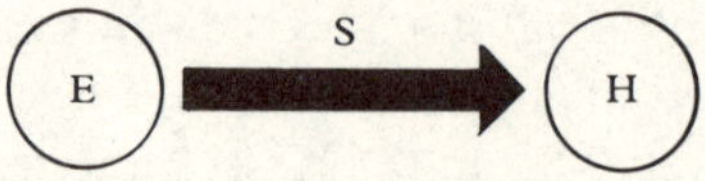

configuring VAXs, which as I mentioned was very successful, we might have something which says:

IF the current context is assigning devices to UNIBUS modules,

   AND we have an unassigned dual port disk drive we know the controller requires,

   AND there are two controllers and neither has any devices already attached to it,

   AND we know how many they can have attached,

THEN assign a disk drive to each of the controllers and note that they have been associated.

So this is a very hard and fast rule. This is prescriptive. It tells you what to do. In fact that's how it's used because it's used to configure the VAXs.

A MYCIN rule might look something like:

IF we're talking about the blood,

   AND we don't already know what the thing is [there's really no point in guessing about it if we already know what it is!],

   AND we know that it is gram negative,

   AND it's rod shaped

   AND the patient has been burned,

THEN we have weak evidence that the identity of the organism is pseudomonas.

Now here we're seeing some uncertainty creep in.

PROSPECTOR takes the notion of a probabilistic rule one step further and provides two numbers. In PROSPECTOR we might

Figure 5.4: Networks of rules

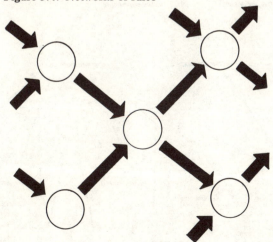

have a rule that says "IF hornblende is pervasively altered to biotite THEN there is strong evidence for potassium zone alteration". The "strong evidence" comes from a large parameter supplied with the rule. A second (in this case, small) number says what to do if the evidence is negative. If there is no hornblende pervasively altered to biotite then the second number is significant, and the small size of that number means that if we don't see it we don't care. In this case a negative piece of evidence doesn't really say anything to us. A positive piece of evidence is something very nice to have. PROSPECTOR differentiated between positive and negative types of statements.

Now as I mentioned we can chain these together. Figure 5.5 is a piece of a PROSPECTOR model from the Porphyry Copper Deposit Type A model, and it includes a number of interesting features. It allows logical combinations here, ANDs and ORs. It provides what's

Figure 5.5: Combining evidence

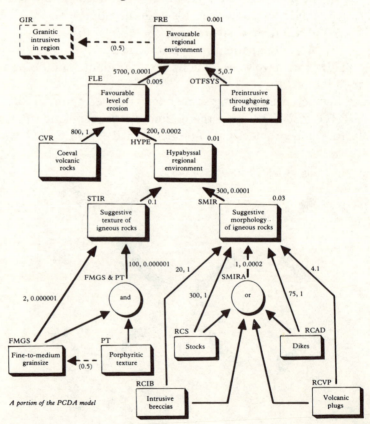

A portion of the PCDA model

called a context mechanism, which prevents it from asking certain questions before other questions have already been answered. It also shuts off certain questions after other questions have been answered. If you have told it pyrite is present you don't want it to come back and ask if there is any evidence of sulphide in the area. Typically we would like our expert systems to sound expert when we are using them. When they ask stupid questions it makes us wonder a little bit.

This is just a portion of the model and putting information in at one of the lower points will typically propagate upward and push up or push down the likelihood of one or the other of the possible deposits. We actually have a model similar to this that we use for selecting the appropriate models in the first place. It asks, "What are we talking about here, are we are talking about copper or are we talking about zinc, molybdenum, or that sort of thing?"

Figure 5.6: A dependency graph

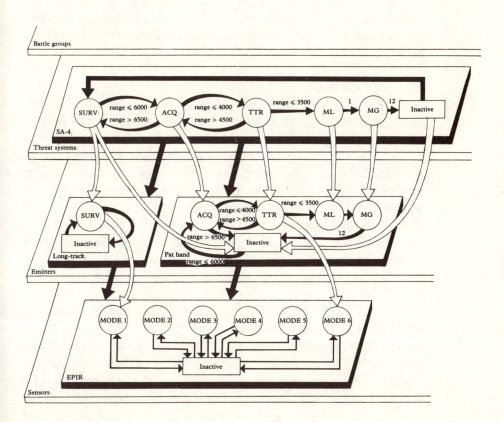

Figure 5.6 is an example of a dependency graph. It illustrates an organisation of knowledge on several levels. Where the top level relates to groups of things, the next to smaller systems, the next level relates to emitters associated with certain of the systems, (radars, etc.) with the last level representing the sensors that we have available. This is part of a system that was used to detect and identify enemy radars. We typically had a number of sensors that we might like to use at any particular instance, and we had models here of what information the sensors could give us. One of the interesting things about this approach is we could put process information into the model. So we can say if this system is doing this, here's what we expect will happen next, or as time passes here's what will happen. We can include temporal functions. In fact these are implicitly temporal in that they are measuring the perceived range to the site which is a function of time because we are moving. We use this sort of structure to put information in at essentially any level. We might have a pilot insert information at one level and we want to be able to propagate in all the directions. We are in some sense accumulating evidence for one of these threats being present. The whole theory that surrounds this is called evidential reasoning which I will allude to just briefly below.

5.5   Inference

We need then to be able to use an input system to somehow combine new information with the knowledge we already have to extend our knowledge base, and "create" new knowledge. The new data enters the inference system. The inference system examines what might be considered long term memory or generic knowledge and produces an instantiated subset of that suggesting its view of what's going on. This goes into a short term memory and creates a view of the situation. The user typically is viewing what's going on in the short term memory. In some sense we can imagine what we are doing is we are transferring instances of knowledge from long term memory to the short term memory, so we are instantiating our knowledge base.

What we would like to do of course is make this loop back from short term memory back into the long term memory. Now this is called learning and as we all know I am sure learning is something we don't do very well in AI, although we have lots of theories about how to do it. This is one area that probably that is going to be critical for real advances in expert systems. The ability for the system to acquire information on its own to generalise from things that it's seen and to add new statements to its long term knowledge base.

Well, as Robert Moore has noted in Chapter 3 there are a number of approaches for drawing inferences from the structures. One way is called *data directed forward chaining*. We put data in at the bottom and it propagates through our structure towards the top. This is the standard way of acquiring evidence, inputting evidence and updating our beliefs about what is going on. In PROSPECTOR this would be taken from the interview with the prospector. He would put in all his findings and then PROSPECTOR would examine its top level goals and decide what it wanted to ask him questions about. This leads to the second notion of *goal directed backward chaining*.

So we may start off with a session (the consultation session) where the user is just putting information in. We've updated the likelihoods of some of the hypotheses which may be that there are ore bodies present. Now we want to ask certain questions to disambiguate, to distinguish, to verify or to refute some of these hypothesis. The question is, "What question do we want to ask?"

Now in PROSPECTOR the approach used is essentially an information theoretic approach. This says supposing we knew that the evidence for these hypotheses was true, what does that do to our current belief? Or suppose we knew they were false? In a sense what it is doing is computing an entropy like measure that it can use to decide

Figure 5.7: The inference system

Task: combine information with knowledge to create "new" knowledge.

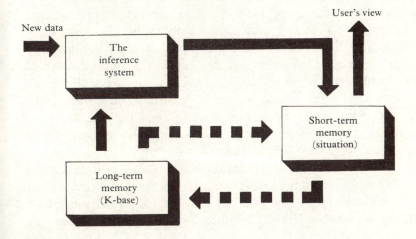

which question it wants to ask. So it will work its way down the structure saying "Well if this were true, if I could verify or refute this would it have a major impact on this node?" Then I recursively ask the same question: 'What's going to have the most effect on my belief here?' Eventually we will get down to some question that can be actually be asked of the user.

Now there are a number of meta control issues that come in here. How do we control this inference process? One is the use of the context relations noted above which force certain questions to be answered before other questions. Another is meta rules where a rule may say if you want to answer this type of question use this set of rules. Mixed initiative is another meta control issue. While the system is working its way down to decide to ask a question, the user may have been thinking himself and have come up with a new question he wants to ask, or new information that he wants to insert. Mixed initiative interactions allow the user to interrupt what the system is doing to say, "Oh, by the way I forgot to tell you I saw this", or "By the way, what about this?" or "Why are you asking that question?" In systems like MYCIN a tremendous amount of complex structure came along with the question, and it was, therefore, very difficult to unwind in order to allow mixed initiative. PROS-PECTOR was set up specifically to allow this sort of interaction, which tends to be the kind of interaction you would have with an expert, he's about to tell you something, you interrupt him and say "Wait a minute, wait a minute, this is what we see."

Supporting opportunistic methods is another meta control issue. With the dependency graph, typically, it is the case that you frequently cannot say in advance what will be evidence and what will be a hypothesis. It may be that you'll acquire either one of the pieces of information first and want to infer the other. Now in many systems, and PROSPECTOR is one of them, if you put in something like that you would have a loop. Now PROSPECTOR, as a matter of fact, doesn't mind having these things in it. Of course it will give you wrong answers but it has no particular bias against them. The difficulty with systems like this is that if you put a little bit of information into a loop, it propagates around and around. It will usually converge, but it will usually not converge to a number like zero or one, which would be an immediate indication that there was a problem. It will converge to some number which is a function of prior probabilities and the topology of the network, etc., which might look entirely reasonable, but won't be. So the ability to turn the inferencing around is critical for lots of situations and one of the reasons why such highly structured and directed systems don't work so well.

Another issue in meta control is the acquisition of information. In PROSPECTOR all the methods for acquiring information are embedded in the structure. It works its way down and it finally gets to a node which has a question associated with it that can be asked of the user. In other systems you might like to have something that steps outside the framework and says what resources do I have for answering questions now? What are they good for? What is their reliability? How expensive are they to use? And wind up making a resource allocation scheme that gets the information by some more direct manner. This is what we've called active acquisition of information and it's in keeping with the notion of a perceptual system that has to actively acquire information about its environment. Systems such as PROSPECTOR are not very good for that kind of thing except when used as small modules of a larger system. Other systems have been much more successful in that area.

As we propagate information, what we are really trying to do is to change the values of probabilities attached to the hypotheses. We have a number of ways of updating these things. The first is by using logic. If A implies B is true and A is true, then we can infer B is true also. If we have a Boolean system that's exactly what we would like to do. Other approaches require that we have some notion of uncertainty, and that gets us into the realm of probability. PROSPECTOR actually uses a conditional probability approach. We start off with some information which indicates the probability associated with the evidence. We have information attached with the rule, which associates conditional probabilities to the hypothesis given the evidence and the hypothesis given the negation of the evidence, and from these we can compute a new probability for the hypothesis. Now in order to do this we typically have to have a prior probability for the evidence, a prior probability for the hypothesis and the conditional probabilities.

There are variants on this, which are also used in PROSPECTOR, which enable you to combine information from several evidence nodes, to arrive at a likelihood for the hypothesis. Now these are typically extensions of standard Bayesian probability. They usually require some sort of notion of independence, which is a difficulty since of course very few of these things are independent – that's why we're doing this. We're looking for dependencies.

Some people have described these approaches as "*ad hoc*", but there's a fellow in our group who refers to them as "odd hack" approaches which I think is probably more to the point.

The Shafer–Dempster (1976) formalism is a relatively new formalism for combining information about likelihoods of events and I'll mention it very briefly (see also Lowrance 1982 and Garvey *et al.* 1981). It's something that we've been working on for quite a while at SRI, but first I'd like to discuss some of the practical difficulties of Bayesian updating. The first problem is that we usually don't have the data that's really necessary in order to do true Bayesian updating. We don't know the priors, and are forced to estimate them. Typically we have no idea, for example, what the prior probability of Joe's being in a certain location might be. To have a real Bayesian system, we also have to estimate all the marginal probabilities. What are the joint probabilities? What are the conditionals? When we are willing to estimate what the prior probability is, then we have the difficulty that these estimates tend to dominate the computations from then on. You'd like it that when you're forced to say something about the priors, they go away as soon as some other information comes in.

The model is difficult to change for these reasons. If you change the probability on one node then in a sense you are affecting the entire model. They are all tightly intertwined.

The computations we use for Bayesian analysis typically give us false precision. We get numbers out. What's the probability that there's gold here? Well, its .0137892. What does that mean? Well, it means there's probably no gold there. The system's carrying these things out to excrutiating detail and some people actually believe the numbers that come out and that's sometimes a difficulty.

Bayesian probabilities tend to be the wrong language for many kinds of knowledge sources. If you want to input information in a Bayesian system, then you're forced to say things about the smallest element in the system – the atomic mutually exclusive events. So for instance, if you have a sensor or something that says an automobile just passed by. Maybe you're interested in what kind of automobile just passed by. Now typically you'd have to make some assumption based on a uniformity principle or something like that and say, well the probability that an automobile just passed by is .6. It could be one of these three cars, so the probability of any one of those .2. Now that's a great leap of faith, because you don't really have any reason whatsoever to say that it's .2. All you can really say is that for any one of those the probability could be up to .6. Because of the mechanics of the computation you're forced to make these more precise statements when you don't really have the information. Once again they hang around, you tend to forget that the reason that it is so precise is that the machine had to make a guess in order to do the arithmetic.

Finally, it is very difficult to distinguish between ignorance and disbelief. If I have assigned a low probability to Joe being in the coffee shop, does that mean that I don't have any particular reason to believe that he is in the coffee shop? Or does it mean that I went and looked and he wasn't there? Those are two rather distinct states of knowledge and typically we would like to be able to keep them separate and its very difficult sometimes in a Bayesian system.

Well, now after having disparaged Bayes I'll mention that Shafer–Dempster formalism fills in some of the gaps in the Bayesian theory. It's a departure from Bayesian probabilities which allows belief to be distributed over propositions which can be supersets of the atomic propositions. So you can actually say something like the probability of it being an automobile is .6, without being forced to make a more precise statement about it. The system will keep track of these superset/subset relations and provide information appropriately. In fact the information, the numbers it provides, are in the form of intervals which show what the constraints are on the actual probability based on the information that you have put in. It's keeping track of notions like ignorance and disbelief and that sort of thing. At the low end of the interval we represent the amount of support for the proposition, how likely is it. At the high end how plausible is it given support for competing propositions. The formation can be used to suspend belief altogether. We can say "I don't know." What that means is it could be anything, and in some sense that places all the belief at the highest level and until you have more information it will stay up there.

The Shafer–Dempster formalism provides two distinct formal techniques. One is for pooling bodies of knowledge (Dempster's Rule) and the other is for extending bodies of knowledge, for drawing implications. Now in most expert systems these are combined into a single technique. For example, in PROSPECTOR, the pooling of new information and the extension of that information to dependent propositions are all combined into one technique. If we have the right structure for a true Bayesian system, then the Shafer–Dempster formalism will do the right thing, and will give you the right Bayesian numbers back. On the other hand, if we have a Boolean system where everything was either true or false, it also does the right thing because of its inference rules.

5.6   User I/O

Most expert systems are required to have some type of explanation capability if they are going to be taken seriously. This is usually in some sort of natural language. Mixed initiative is very important just because it gives a more natural feel to the consultation and graphical I/O is typically very important, but it's really a function of the application that the thing is being used for.

The type of interaction that PROSPECTOR allowed was very natural for the geologists. Geologists usually don't want to sit down in front of a terminal and start typing in natural language or anything else. They are used to using maps. They like to draw things and like to say, you know, here's the outline of a certain sort of chemical structure. Here are faults and intrusions and all sorts of things like that. They come back with these maps that are all drawn scrawled up.

What we'd like to be able to do is use these directly. In PROSPECTOR we allowed this possibility by providing a map input mechanism where PROSPECTOR would go through and compute the favourability for certain sorts of ore bodies at every point. So if you thought of the map as an image then at every pixel we would be asking, "What's the favourability?" So we allow the user to input his map data by drawing "images". The user can provide information about structures, metals found in the area, the geothermal properties, and other sorts of structures that are particularly interesting to him by just outlining them.

Finally, PROSPECTOR will come back and show the current favourability, by expressing it graphically using a pseudo-colour rendition. This approach was used to input the assays where the large molybdenum deposit was really discovered. The area with the highest concentration was, ironically enough, where the mining company was already planning to dig. They already had intentions to mine, and they weren't looking for molybdenum. In fact the high molybdenum region was where they were planning to put waste from the mine that they were going to dig. My understanding is they are still planning to do so, so maybe they are not so impressed by $100,000,000 worth of molybdenum or maybe it cost $101,000,000 to get it out. Anyway it turned out that the area which was predicted by PROSPECTOR to be high molybdenum was in fact high molybdenum. To the geologist the graphical interface was exactly what they were used to and looking for. It was a very natural interface for them. There are a variety of other sorts of graphic interfaces of that sort which are natural for other users and wherever possible you would like to use them.

5.7 System development

The typical stages in knowledge engineering are: problem identification, conceptualisation, formalisation, implementation, and testing. You start off trying to figure out what the problem that you are trying to solve really is. You conceptualise an approach for how to solve that problem. For example, you sit down with the geologist and find out from him what he thought was important. You put together a conceptual model of what he just said and by iteration get some agreement. Next you formalise that model, perhaps in terms of production rules or some other method, and implement it on the computer.

Once you've implemented it you can begin testing it and the knowledge acquisition system for PROSPECTOR, for example, enabled very easy testing. You could put in information and interactively try things out and test the validity of certain assumptions. Once you decided you really liked it, then you could do sensitivity analyses and all sorts of tests to see just how well it really worked. Any one of these steps should be considered to have feedback loops to any of the previous steps in this process. After testing you may decide that it was the wrong problem that was identified here and you are back at Square 1.

Now this is a standard approach to engineering an expert system. It probably should look familiar, because I could just as easily have described software development in the same words, and in fact they are the same. This is how we write a program, we try to figure out what it is we are writing the program about and so forth. In effect my view of expert systems these days is they provide an extension to our current programming techniques. They provide a method by which we can express things that are more complex or express things more transparently than we were able to before, in more standard languages such as LISP or PASCAL or PROLOG, certainly than in PROLOG.

There are a number of tools available these days, and more are coming at a prodigious rate. M1 and S1 come from Teknowledge. KEE is from Intellicorp. GRASPER is a tool we're using at SRI, and was implemented by John Lowrance. ART is a tool put out by Inference Corporation. These things typically enable you to view the structures that you're working with, see what information is relevant to them, do little experiments, that sort of thing. Watch the system when it's actually operating. Most of them run with the exception perhaps of M1 on serious machines, such as LISP machines and that sort of thing.

There are certain keys to building a successful expert system. First of all you should choose a problem that has an available expert. It's nice if the expertise that the expert has is also available but that's not always the case. Certainly we're probably all experts in seeing. We're experts in walking up stairs and outdoors and things like that. That's very difficult to impart to a machine.

You should provide the right tools to a knowledge engineer to develop the system. Most importantly, though, is to set realistic objectives for ourselves. It won't do to expect that a novice is going to come in and encode your expertise and produce wonders in an expert system. Despite everything that you've heard about it, it just doesn't happen. If you think of these things as extensions of programming languages then this is not unreasonable. You have to be a fairly competent programmer to produce wonders from any other programming language and novices typically don't do that.

Your objectives should be incremental. You should be able to see some sort of success early on. If you have to wait for five years of development to turn on the system and see if it works, it's highly unlikely anyone is going to give you the leeway to do that. You've got to be producing as you go and while that's really more of a management issue it's extremely important. So you must plan for an evolutionary development, with some near term wins as you proceed toward your far term goals. Particularly, as most of the far term goals are far too grandiose for success in current expert systems. The sociological and the technology transfer issues are every bit as important as the technology base these days. That's where things like graphical interfaces and opimised man–machine interfaces really come into play. I think they're the key to making a successful expert system.

So if you see an ad that says, for instance, "the feature of this knowledge base, of this system, is that you get knowledge engineering in hours and not years", or "knowledge can be maintained by secretaries and not experts, and knowledge workstations can be gotten with an entry level price of less than $5,000", be very careful! These quotes were in a brochure that I picked up at the American Association for Artificial Intelligence (AAAI) Conference last year. "Knowledge maintenance by secretaries not experts", if true, suggests that perhaps your secretary should be doing your job if that's really the case. You're wasting her, or him, as your secretary.

If you see ads like that, ask to see the system. What is the knowledge that's being maintained here, is it inputting a bunch of numbers, or is it changing rules around? I would be willing to bet that the knowledge maintained here is somebody sitting down and typing in today's stock quotations or something like that which is definitely stretching a point.

The current state of the art is that we get pretty good performance in very limited domains. If the knowledge can be represented well by definitions and categories of things, discrete descriptions and relatively simple non-interacting rules, then we can do a pretty good job on it. Particularly if the paradigms for using the knowledge are also fairly simple. Forward or backward chaining, filling out forms or filling in slots, simple deductions and very simple search methods. Once again if the models that we're using are relatively simple, discrete, bounded and maybe factorable into small modules. I would say expert systems these days are still relatively "researchy". It takes a lot of work to bring up an expert system that's of any competence.

5.8   Areas for IKBS research

There are several areas for future research in expert systems. Certainly research in representation schemes is something that is likely to pay off. We don't represent time very well. We typically don't use the notion of processes that vary over time. We're not even sure what a belief is although we can talk about likelihood and that sort of stuff. We need a computationally effective notion of modality.

If we really want to be expert we need to have techniques for controlling very, very large knowledge bases. Most expert systems use a relatively small knowledge base. In order to control them we have to have methods for abstracting from large knowledge bases to smaller more manageable knowledge bases. We need to be able to trade off shallow reasoning using surface properties, and deep reasoning using causal relationships. We need to be able to resolve conflicts and inconsistencies in a knowledge base, and we need to be able to deal with multiple views of a knowledge base and multiple representations of the same knowledge. We need better techniques for controlling inference.

That's not all, other areas that are important are ways of having distributed expertise, distributed problem solvers, multiple experts. As most of you know, if you get two experts together and try to find some sort of consensus it is very difficult, most experts don't agree with one another for some reason.

We need to be able to deal with dependent evidence. Almost all of our evidence is really dependent in some sense. We need to be able to recognise dependencies and know how to factor them out and handle them.

We need better techniques for knowledge acquisition. We need I believe better techniques for commonsense reasoning if we ever want to see real experts.

5.9   Conclusions

Given all that I'd say there're still many opportunities. People are writing working expert systems for medical problems, equipment trouble shooting (that will probably actually be a fairly high pay off and it's nice because to a certain extent you can constrain the set of possibilities). They will be used as modules within other systems that are supposed to be intelligent; robotic systems, planning systems, etc. The military will probably use them. They're certainly paying money to buy them. There are certain military operations which are amenable to expert systems. They'll be used for the design of chips to support expert systems. I really liked Mark Stefik's thesis some years ago. He developed MOLGEN, which was an expert system for designing genetic experiments, I thought here we're really getting to self replicating systems. It hasn't quite got to that point yet, but we've come a long way.

References and suggestions for further reading

Duda, R.O., Gaschnig, J.G. & Hart P.E. (1979). Model design in the PROS-PECTOR consultant system for mineral exploration. In *Expert systems in the Microelectronic Age*, ed. D Michie, pp. 153–167. Edinburgh: Edinburgh University Press.

Garvey, T.D., Lowrance, J.D. & Fischler, M.A. (1981). An inference technique for integrating knowledge from disparate sources. In *Proceedings of the International Joint Conference on Artificial Intelligence*. Vancouver, British Columbia, Canada: University of British Columbia, pp. 319–325.

Lowrance, J.D. (1982). Dependency-graph models of evidential support. Amherst, Massachusetts: Ph.D. dissertation, Department of Computer and Information Science, University of Massachusetts.

McDermott, J. (1980). R1: An expert in the computer systems domain. In *Proceedings of the National Conference of the American Association for Artificial*

Intelligence. Stanford, California: Stanford University, pp. 269–271.
Shafer, G. (1976). *A Mathematical Theory of Evidence*. Princeton: Princeton University Press.
Shortliffe, E.H., Buchanan, B.G. & Feigenbaum, E.A. (1979). Knowledge engineering for medical decision making: A review of computer-based clinical decision aids. *Proceedings of the IEEE*, Vol. 67 pp. 1207–1224.

6

MICHAEL MELLIAR-SMITH

Software technology and the new techniques

6.1 Introduction

At SRI we have been working with formal methods for the development of computer systems and rather particularly with the formal specification and rigorous mechanical verification of the design of those systems. As an example of the kind of thing that we do in that area, I will tell you about a specific system for which I was involved in some verification work – SIFT, a reliable aircraft control computer. SIFT stands for Software Implemented Fault Tolerance.

The problem we had with SIFT was that the Federal Aviation Authority, for whatever reason, had expressed a reliability requirement of one failure per million years of operation. That requirement has nothing to do with the safety of the passengers; they drive to the airport on the freeway and that's much more hazardous. Of course you can't go out and measure that kind of reliability; you have to extrapolate it from something that is more conveniently measured, and then you have the problem of whether or not your extrapolation has any meaning. We needed to provide some form of rigorous justification of the means we used to extrapolate to that reliability figure, to show that it had some relevance to the actual system. We ended up doing a relatively interesting mathematical proof, you could call it a proof of design correctness, to try to justify what we were doing. To do the proof, we used the kind of techniques of formal specification and mechanical verification that we have been developing.

I'm not going to talk in this essay about fifth generation systems very much because I'm not quite certain that I really know very much about fifth generation systems. I'm not going to talk about the tools that you would use to build a fifth generation system because I don't really know what they would be. I will talk about tools that we have at the moment, and tools that would be based on formal techniques of the kind I'm familiar with. Most of those tools are not yet very good, so I really would not recommend your using them at present. What I really want to talk about are the kind of tools that we might run on a fifth generation computer system. These are tools that are not available at present, and thus you'll have to take much of what I say with a pinch of salt.

The Computer Science Laboratory at SRI is just one floor up from the Artificial Intelligence Center, and we have good relations with them and a certain friendly rivalry. If they discover anything that we like, we try to steal it of course claiming it to be Computer Science. We like to say that their interest is in artificial intelligence and we depend upon the natural variety. When I say that I think that I want to emphasise that we mean a little bit more than just claiming that we use intelligence, and much of what I want to talk about is taking advantage of the intelligence of the users of your systems.

6.2   Systems to support the expert user

A part of the problem that Stan Rosenschein has when he sets out to build an R2D2 or an equivalent is that this robot he is building, or his natural language understanding system, necessarily has to be substantially self contained. The kind of systems in which I am interested work with a user and I do not have the requirement that my system is entirely automatic, that it can work independently of a user. Consequently, I have a certain advantage; I can perhaps make things work that would be difficult to make work otherwise. Thus the topic I want to cover is *systems to support the expert user*.

By an expert user, I think mostly about programmers and system designers; those are the expert users with which I am most familiar. But, to take another example, I could be thinking perhaps of an economist trying to predict the behaviour of the economy. He is undoubtedly an expert user and we would like to provide him with tools that support the kind of predictions he is trying to achieve and these tools of course are very non-trivial kind of tools. We know how successful the current rate of achievement is on that topic.

To support the expert user we can say that our system:

▶ must communicate in the user's language domain
▶ must be predictable
▶ must be responsive.

You are probably feeling that all of this is indeed motherhood and it is motherhood. The problem is that it is not necessarily easy. We should think about which of these topics is the most difficult. One might say that communicating in the user's language is a difficult topic, and indeed a lot of work and a lot of system software engineering go into communicating with users in their language domain. One might worry about performance. Well, fortunately I am talking some years into the future when Professor Aiso has delivered his machine. So performance might not be so much of a problem as now, although it's definitely something we have to worry about. The real problem that causes so much difficulty in this topic is the problem of obtaining predictability in the behaviour of these complicated tools.

Now when you bring a novice user to the computer, the novice user is confronted with a system that doesn't talk in his language, which he doesn't understand and which doesn't necessarily respond to the commands he gives. And sometimes it does. Too often a novice user tends to think in terms of some repertoire of magic incantations which make the system do limited things, because that is the only form of understanding that he can achieve of the behaviour of the computer system. I need not tell you that this is very destructive of his ability to use the system effectively, and it is extremely frustrating to the user.

Unfortunately, this problem of magic incantations and the resulting frustration is not just limited to novice users. A couple of weeks ago, I was fortunate in being able to experiment with a natural language system, not the one designed at SRI. The system is really quite an impressive system. Within a minute or so trying my hand at it, I was able to make it answer a number of queries entirely correctly and quite naturally. Of course, I then thought a bit and in the next minute or so I was able to persuade it to answer a number of further queries incorrectly.

The basic problem of course is that the natural language system has certain limitations. They are limitations that were not fully explained or documented, and that the system was not capable of recognising itself. Whereas it didn't take me very long to actually provoke a query which caused it to come to grief, it might take a normal user rather longer, and he would not expect to run into this problem every minute. But, on the other hand, if you are using a natural language query system and you have an uneasy feeling that, even maybe once a day, it is going to give you a wrong answer for reasons that you do not understand and which the system is not capable of recognising and warning you, then you are going to have very uncomfortable feelings about your relationship with that system.

Here is another example of this, from my own personal experience with a real tool that I was trying to use myself. It concerns a proof system that we were trying to use to do the proof work on the SIFT system. We were trying to use a mechanical verifi·ation system, that is probably the most sophisticated automatic mechanical verification system in the world even now. In its way a very excellent, beautifully engineered piece of software engineering, a real work of art.

In trying to use that verification system, I had two problems, one of which was that the language domain wasn't the language domain that I wanted to use. The system worked in the domain of recursive function theory, and that was rather a restricted domain for what I wanted to say. We could have lived with that restriction; the problem that caused us to come to grief was that, in order to attempt to be entirely automatic which it did not succeed in being, the system naturally contained interesting heuristics. A true piece of artificial intelligence programming, it had these beautifully designed internal heuristics to attempt to do proofs which you could not reasonably expect to be done without these heuristics. Of course, sometimes the heuristics worked and sometimes they didn't. I and my colleague didn't want to understand how the internal mechanism of this thing worked, and thus it was a complete mystery to us when and why these heuristics actually operated, and what was the appropriate thing to say in any particular circumstance. It was extremely frustrating for us, exactly the same kind of feeling that your novice user has when he first confronts the computer. We didn't understand how it worked internally, we didn't know what to say to make it work. Sometimes we said "A and B implies C" and the proof would fail, but if we had said "B and A implies C" it would have worked, and how were we to know what to say?

The conclusion we came to at that time was that magic was really very frustrating. For users of computers *magic is not the answer*. It is very important to avoid it. As a result of that frustrating experience, we then built a different kind of system, a system of the kind that I want to talk about. We were able to do the work that we had to do with a system which was designed to attempt to support us as users rather than to attempt to be automatic.

We start with the idea of predictability. Our user is an expert user, he knows what he is doing, he knows the field completely, he understands what it is he wants the computer to do, he knows what it is that the computer is capable of doing by itself, what it is not capable of doing by itself, and what he is going to have to help the computer with. All of this, of course, has to be expressed in terms that this expert user is going to be familiar with and comfortable with.

But your expert user in general is not going to be a computer scientist, and that is not a requirement of the verification system that we are building. The expert user may be willing to learn a certain amount and you can get away with stylised languages, but it all has to be in the domains with which he is familiar and happy.

Thus the question is that we have the expert user and we have the computer and we have to build a system that does useful non-trivial things and still behaves in an entirely predictable manner to that user. The technique which we came up with, and which we are advocating, is a technique of building the system in terms of decision procedures for decidable domains.

6.3   Decision procedures for decidable domains

For those of you who are not magicians, I will explain for a moment what a decision procedure is. Basically, it is a mechanical algorithm, the kind of thing that computers do well, for deciding whether some proposition is true or false. One can talk also about semi decision procedures which will say, perhaps, yes, it's true or will go on computing and searching and trying to find out whether it's true indefinitely. If a semi decision procedure does not stop you still don't know whether the result is false or whether it maybe just hasn't quite reached the decision point yet. One would really prefer to have straight decision procedures which will say definitely yes or no.

Another point of importance is the requirement for responsiveness. There are many domains for which, in principle, we could build the decision procedure but the computational cost is so high that it is not really effective.

Our experience with the very preliminary prototypes that we have of this kind of a system indicates that we must preserve the concentration of the expert user on the problem at hand. If we permit the computer to compute by itself for more than about one minute, we start to lose the concentration of our expert user. Responsiveness matters in terms of preserving the concentration of the user.

Consequently, we must think in terms of systems which have realistic performance properties. Even with fifth generation computers, the performance problem is not entirely alleviated. One can have fast computers, one can have hundreds of these fast computers, if you believe they are going to be that cheap, and if you can afford to make a considerable capital investment to support your expert user. But the computation costs of some of these decision procedures are not merely exponential on the size of the problem, they are sometimes even exponential of an exponential in complexity. That gets pretty big pretty quickly, and thus large increases in computer power can yield only small increases in the complexity of the problems that can be solved.

My attitude to fast computers is like the attitude of the Texas cowhand with a big thirst who was of the opinion that nowhere in the world, not even in Texas, did there exist such a thing as a large whisky. For the building of decision procedures, there is no such thing as a fast computer.

Propositional calculus. An example of a domain in which we can build a decision procedure is propositional calculus, a somewhat restricted version of predicate calculus, lacking the 'for all' and the 'exists'. The advantage of removing those from the predicate calculus is that it allows us to have a decision procedure. The disadvantage is that it restricts what we can say.

Pressberger arithmetic. Another decidable domain is Pressberger arithmetic, a somewhat restricted form of arithmetic. No doubt, it would be very popular in the schools. It has addition, subtraction, greater than, and less than, and it has multiplication only by known integer constants. The reason why you can have multiplication by known integer constants is that you can do it by repeated addition.

Equalities and inequalities. We also have a decision procedure for equality and inequality that can operate on uninterpreted functions, that does not need to know what kind of values it is operating on. Equality and inequality will work on anything, whereas, of course, propositional calculus is only for boolean propositions, and Pressberger arithmetic is for numbers.

You note that there are three decision procedures there. The question arises as to whether or not they can be made to cooperate with each other and the answer to that is yes they can, and indeed they don't even need to know about each other. We have been able to build these procedures so that we can add on further decision procedures in a really quite modular manner and they fit together and work together really quite well.

What use are we going to make of these decision procedures? The basic advantage of a decision procedure is that in that domain, the decidable domain, you can ask a question and the decision procedure will tell you yes or no. It will definitely produce a result. It is not a question of whether you ask the question correctly. If the question is in the domain, you will get your answer. But you can also do much more than that. Because you have this kind of deductive capability, you can then do interesting things with it.

6.4   Tools for decidable theories

As an example of a useful domain we have Horn-clause logic, which is an even more restricted form of logic than the propositional calculus, and is the underlying logical theory of PROLOG. PROLOG was subsequently embellished, and it is not restricted just to the pure logical domain of Horn-clauses now. But the origins of PROLOG, and particularly the ability to develop the PROLOG compiler, depend upon the decidability of Horn-clauses.

Another example, less obvious perhaps, is LR1 context free grammars, a very elegantly decidable domain that enables us to produce parser generators. I don't think many people write parsers from scratch nowadays. That's because we now have a good tool to produce parsers with, and the tool exists because we can express our grammars in a domain in which we can provide the kind of mechanical support that we would like to provide.

Type checking for languages is also decidable, and not terribly complicated. We can build ourselves mechanical typecheckers for programming languages and these are useful to programmers. They find errors which would otherwise have to be found by more difficult and tedious debugging techniques.

A more advanced decidable domain is Eqlog, a language that Joe Goguen has been designing at SRI. A part of the characteristics of this language is that, in a certain sense, you can get full coverage test case generators for that language. Eqlog does have very nice characteristics in terms of trying to construct this kind of testing tool, which is a kind of tool that you would like to have, a useful tool that becomes feasible if you are working in the appropriate kind of logical domain.

In principle, everything that the computer does is a decision procedure. There is nothing a computer does that isn't in fact a mechanical algorithm for deciding something or other. The qualification is that *the decidable domain is not useful to you, unless you can explain it to the user in his own terms.* When we produce a horrible, complicated piece of computer software, of the kind that regretably is only too common, that piece of software is still a decision procedure. Unfortunately it might be very difficult to explain to the user what it was that you are actually basing your decision on – what the decidable domain was. So we must not only have a decidable domain and decision procedure for it, but we have to be able to explain it to the user. The user has to understand what the decidable domain is so that he can be confident that he is within that decidable domain.

If we take that little example of the natural language system with which I was playing, undoubtedly the natural language system had some underlying theories and was not entirely arbitrary. They didn't care to explain to me what the underlying theory was of course, and it would have been hard for them to explain it to me in my own uneducated natural language terms. They were not checking themselves to see that they were staying within that domain, and that is where they came to grief. Had they been willing to explain to the users what they could understand and what they couldn't understand and had they then checked to see that they were indeed staying within the domain of the things that they understood and recognised when they went out of it, then I would not have been in a position to provoke the system into producing incorrect answers.

One of our problems, of course, is that decidable domains are quite restricted. They are narrow, logical domains. A broad and interesting domain, the kind of domain that is needed for general applications, is almost certain to be undecidable. Purely mechanical support, without any human intervention, is not effective for these interesting domains. The combinatorial complexity is too high and the heuristics sometimes work and sometimes don't work. But we are not in that situation, for we have the advantage of having an expert user to help us. Thus the question is, how are we going to take advantage of the help of that expert user.

In Figure 6.1, the outer domain is the domain of full user language, the domain in which our expert user expresses his understanding of the problem, and inside we have the more limited decidable domain, a narrow restricted domain that can be mechanically processed. For a verification system, the statements of interest are boolean propositions. Some proportion of the statements that can be made in the language are valid and of course some of them are not valid. We need the verification system to confirm that our theorems are valid, but for the full language that cannot be decided mechanically. The expert user is able to recognise that the theorem is outside the decidable domain, because the decidable domain can be simply explained to him, and can provide us with advice that carries the theorem inside the decidable domain where the mechanical decision process is effective. It is very important that the manner in which the advice is given is such that theorems that are valid mapped into theorems that are still valid, and that theorems that are invalid area map to theorems that are invalid.

Can we build systems in which the advice of the user is entirely in terms of his own original understanding of the domain? The answer is yes; we have built two such systems. These were rather specialised systems in the area of mechanical theorem proving, because we set

Figure 6.1: Application area for systems to support expert users

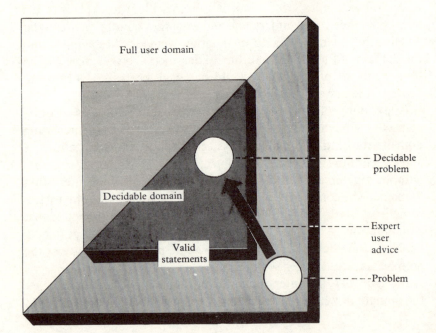

out to build a mechanical theorem prover without understanding in advance that we needed a system to support an expert user. We built the STP theorem prover, which was the one used for the design proof of SIFT and was not a fully engineered system, and we are now building another system which does not have a name yet.

Our new verification system operates in the domain of second order predicate calculus and the communication with the user is in terms of the second order predicate calculus. The second order predicate calculus I need hardly say is not a decidable domain. Yet by providing advice to the system purely in the user's terms, we have been able to use this system to do some non-trivial proofs, particularly, for instance, a proof about the non-existence of cryptoanalytic functions.

Our current system has limitations; it is a very experimental system, very much a prototype. The user has to know what advice to give, but this in fact is possible. The users do indeed know what advice they are required to provide, but our current system is rather tedious to use. Next year we hope to get the system to the point at which the system will ask for advice and will offer choices to the user, again in the terms that the user understands. We hope that it will become a much more convenient kind of system for the users to work with.

It is important to note that use of this system by an expert user depends only on his or her understanding of the domain of knowledge relevant to the application, in this case the second order predicate calculus. You can use this system with the amount of knowledge which you would obtain in an undergraduate course in logic at a university, and without knowing anything else about computer science at all. That is much less knowledge than you would need in order to build the system. The internal structure of the system is indeed complex, but is hidden. This objective is essential if we are going to support expert users in other topics, for example an economist. Such experts are certainly not going to know anything about computer science.

The domain we have discussed so far is a domain within computer science. Can we extend this into application domains without requiring programming in LISP in order to build decision procedures? Indeed, the answer is yes, we can, and this depends on some work which Joseph Goguen has been doing at SRI. I am sure that there are corresponding techniques which would be applicable which have been developed at universities as well. He has been developing a language called Eqlog. It is a language which combines the kind of algebraic specification techniques which John Guttag originated with PROLOG-like clausal reasoning, and it has the kind of characteristics you would hope for. It is a fully typed system; it is modular; the modules are parameterisable, and you can combine them together to produce combination theories.

Eqlog is not a programming language. Eqlog is a logic, and is just exactly what we need in order to build these application domains and to build them in a modular manner. We can also build an interpretative decision procedure that uses Eqlog theories using technology that exists today. With a lot more work, we can build a compiled decision procedure based on the same kind of techniques that are used to build a PROLOG compiler and produce efficient decision procedures if that is appropriate for the application.

A second example of an interesting higher level decidable domain is the domain of interval logic, a decidable logic for reasoning about temporal relations. Figure 6.2 shows a formula and also a graphical representation of that formula. One of the interesting characteristics of interval logic is that the graphical representation, which is very intuitive to users, contains the same information as the formula above it and is just as meaningful to the computer system.

Figure 6.2: Request acknowledgement protocol axioms

Init. $\neg$ R $\wedge$ $\neg$ A

A1. [R $\Rightarrow$ $*$ A] $\neg$ A $\wedge$ $\square$ R

A2. [A $\Rightarrow$ begin $*$ $\neg$ R]R $\wedge$ $\square$ A

A3. [begin $\neg$ R $\Rightarrow$] $*$ $\neg$ A

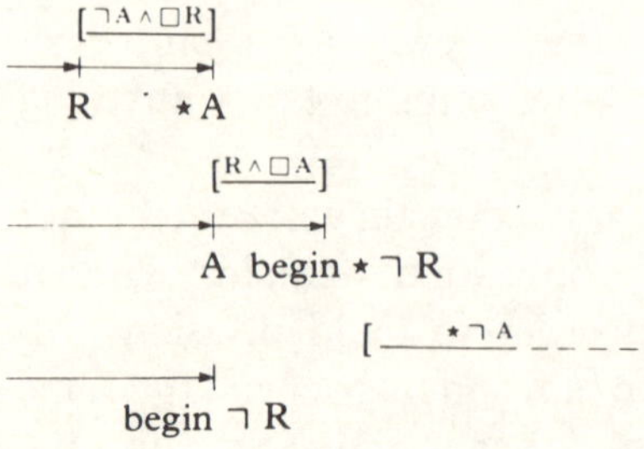

Our aim, we don't have it now but we hope to have it sometime next year, is that you should be able to doodle on the screen and draw pictures like these about the temporal relationships in your system. Because they are very intuitive kind of pictures you can understand them very well, but the system can then go off from your doodles and actually reason about the temporal relationships and maybe prove theorems for you. This kind of human interface is one of our objectives. Unfortunately, there are very few examples of the use of graphics like this in formal computer science.

One of the characteristics of Eqlog which is daunting to unfamiliar users is that Eqlog is very definitely a bottom up tool. It is a tool for use by professional programmers or logicians, or perhaps the knowledge engineer.

Most of the time, however, our users prefer to reason top down rather than bottom up. This is a situation in which we have incomplete information. We don't yet know what we are talking about fully. If we knew what we were talking about, we would probably have written it in a more complete and formal manner. Now we are talking about something in which we have basically only a partial specification of the system we are talking about. We are going to be involved in speculation, we are going to ask "what if", and we are going to elaborate this on the basis of what we can find out about the system.

So, let's start with a little comment about the kinds of situation we are in. If we had written our specification of the system in a language like Eqlog, say, we would have had one model of the system. But that specification would represent one model, an initial model. If we have a partial specification, then of course it admits of a lot of different kinds of models. We have to sort out all of those different models and find out which one or which ones we meant to talk about. So, what we want to do, and we are nowhere near doing this yet, is we want to start with a partial specification and perhaps a speculation about that specification. Then we will build something, a logical structure called a semantic tableau, which basically identifies the possible models for the specification that we have built. Then we are going to factor the tableau to extract various of those possible models and this is not an easy thing to do, because you have in fact to separate things whose relationship to each other is unclear. And then, even more difficult, you are going to have to convert it back into the user domain because when you built the semantic tableau you did it in terms of the underlying logic which you were working in on the machine, and that is not the logic which the user knew anything about. Typically, we aim for something like one or two orders of magnitude expansion from the user's domain into the underlying logic in the machine. So then you have to get rid of that to get back to the user's domain, and that is not easy.

After conversion back to the user's domain, we want to take these models back and ask the user what it is that he wants and what he does not want. As a result of his comments we may augment his specification. For example, the user might present his partial specification to the system, and ask under what circumstances could this be true? The system will scratch its head and say, "well, of course it won't be true if there are no users of the system". And you will say, "well, I don't want to exclude that case, but that wasn't the circumstance I was interested in, so how about trying another one." The system may come back and say, "well, that would be true if user A and user B both had the same password". This is clearly something that you did want to exclude. So then you will start to say something like, well, we will add another thing to our specification. We will say that if user A is not the same as user B, then user A's password is not the same as user B's password and add that into the specification and see what difference that makes and try again. We hope, and this, I assure you, is some distance off in the future, to be able to provide a tool which will allow the user to experiment and refine and elaborate his or her specification at a very abstract level in this kind of a way.

6.5   Conclusions

We have covered in this essay a number of techniques which might be possible within the next decade. What I hoped to demonstrate is that systems to support the expert user are an interesting topic for research, a topic for research on the kind of time scale that we are talking about when we talk of future generations of computers.

References and suggestions for further reading

Goguen, J.A. & Meseguer, J. (1984). Equality, types, modules, and (why not?) generics for logic programming. *Journal of Logic Programming*, Vol. 1, 2, pp. 179–210.
Melliar-Smith, P.M. & Schwartz, R.L. (1982). Formal specification and mechanical verification of SIFT: A fault-tolerant flight control system. *IEEE Transactions on Computers*, C-31, 7, 616–630.

Shostak, R.E., Schwartz, R.L. & Melliar-Smith, P.M. STP: a mechanised logic for specification and verification. *Proceedings of the 6th Conference on Automated Deduction*, 1982, pp. 32–49. Published as: Lecture Notes in Computer Science, #138, Springer-Verlag.

Guttag, J.V. & Horning, J.J. (1978). The algebraic specification of abstract data types. *Acta Informatica*, 10, 1 (1978), 27–52.

7

PROFESSOR ERIK SANDEWALL
System development environments

7.1 Introduction

There is a need to bring about a synthesis of knowledge engineering techniques or expert system techniques on the one hand, and conventional software engineering on the other. This arises from the limited market and limited range of applications for the separate expert system tools that we see today. There would be much more applicability if we could embed intelligent facilities of the type that expert systems provide into conventional software.

My recommendation for how to bring that about is that we should try to *unpackage* expert systems. Instead of buying or building fixed packages which promise to serve as a shell for an expert system, we should look inside them to see what software engineering techniques are being used there. We should then try to apply the same software engineering techniques for more mundane purposes.

In this essay I want to show how that recommendation can be carried out, in the particular context of office systems. I will do this not only as a pedagogical exercise, but also as a report from actual research projects. I have outlined the steps which we have gone through in our own research. We started as an artificial intelligence group quite a number of years ago and in the middle 70's a large part of our group switched its focus to study office systems. So we have been working for a number of years on office systems but from the background and the perspective of artificial intelligence.

7.2   An AI perspective on office systems

The standard computer-based office services are certainly familiar from the literature, and many people today use them in their daily business. There is a need for text editing and handling structured data such as forms, and for various services such as computer mail. The computer calendar is often described and often implemented but apparently not so often used. It is of course an attractive concept in principle. You will also find a need for several more specialised services in each office application of computers, such as mailing lists and various aspects of accounting.

During the first phase of our research, we allowed our software to grow and built up the software that provided these various services in our own working environment. While we did so, we also gradually tried to generalise on the software that was being used. One of the steps that turned out useful was to build a general purpose editor. We called it ED3 because it operated on *tree* structures. (The Swedish language doesn't have the 'th' sound, so 3 and tree sounded similar to us) (Strömfors and Jonesjö 1981).

The idea in ED3 is that, instead of having a text editor, you have an editor which operates on a tree. The user decides how he wants to organise his data in terms of this tree. For example, if you have a large document which is conveniently organised as chapters, sections, and so on, then you would let each of those subdivisions be one part of the tree. If you have a program which has a block structure, then you have a similar natural tree structure in your data.

So one of the two basic parts of the ED3 editor allowed the user to change the structure of a tree: to add, delete, or move whole branches of a tree. The other basic part allowed him to do text editing in the leaves of the trees. Each leaf, or terminal node, of the tree was supposed to be a piece of text. Gradually, as we used it, we recognised that there was a need for other kinds of leaves. Sometimes it was convenient to let one leaf be a figure, a graph, a picture, a table or some other collection of structured data. The number of variants and extensions of this tree editor grew. There was EDG for graphics, EDF for forms and so on, and ED* for the most general system.

Similar ideas have emerged in other places, and are presently becoming popular under the catchword of 'outline processors'.

These general purpose editors capture one key idea in what we think is the key software engineering principle used in AI – always try to write general purpose software that applies to tagged data. Instead of having a number of separate programs, each of which applies to one specific kind of data, we attempt to write one program which is able to cover all those needs, at least when those programs have a similar structure. We organise the data so that local tags specify which specific kind of data occurs in each position.

This might seem like a very simple observation, and it is a very simple observation, but at the same time it does run counter to some of the underlying practices and underlying principles of conventional programming languages. When you start out to write a program in COBOL, PASCAL, or any other conventional programming language, you first write declarations of the data you are going to use. After that, you write procedures which operate relative to the declarations. Your program is therefore tied down to those particular data structures that are expressed in the declarations. If you have a number of different applications which require essentially the same procedures, but different data structures, this programming discipline forces you, or at least strongly encourages you, to write several programs with a similar procedure content.

The alternative is, not to begin by writing the declarations. Instead write the program first, and organise it so that the declarations are variable. This is often an issue which is brought up in the debate about conventional programming languages versus languages such as LISP or PROLOG. The proponents of the classical languages complain about the lack of declarations in, for example, LISP. The answer is that people in the LISP culture certainly see the need for descriptions of the structure of data. That facility is so important that it should not be restricted to be just a constant for a program. It is important to be able to write programs which can accept data descriptions, i.e. the kind of information that you put in declarations, and which can decode those data descriptions. Instead of having fixed declarations *in* the program, we should be able to treat the declarations *as data structures* and let the program decode them.

We then proceeded to examine the specialised services in our office environment. We found some services which could be satisfied in the context of that tree structure editor or outline processor. We took the opportunity to implement various services as far as possible in the uniform environment rather than build special software for it. There were also some applications in the office environment that required more than the general purpose editor could provide. This led us to implement a number of tools for these particular classes of applications (Sandewall 1982).

One very obvious tool was a forms handler, or forms management system. It was of course an example of the principle of writing general software rather than using declarations. A second tool which built on the forms management tool was an information flow handler. The need for this tool was first seen in an application in the university hospital, namely the information traffic between the patient ward and the laboratory for chemical analysis of samples from patients.

Essentially, the patient ward issues purchase requests, internal requests for analysis for each sample that they wanted to have processed. In the daily work of the hospital, this request was issued using forms on paper. The very simple observations we made were that lots of forms are used in organisations, and when you complete a form you almost never proceed to put it in the drawer of your desk. Rather, when you have completed a form you send it on to somebody else. That other person is likely either to add some more information to it and send it on again, or he or she will leave it on his desk for a while and later do something to it, more or less immediately.

If you trace the itineraries that are taken by forms in the organisation, you will see certain standard paths, but also cases where a form goes on a unique route. The degree of standardisation of the itineraries depends on the character of the organisation and the topic that the form addresses. In the particular cases we looked at first, there were very strongly standardised paths for the forms.

They went from the ward where the patient and the doctor were located to the chemical laboratory and from there back to the ward, as well as to central files, to accounting, and so on.

A reasonable way of describing this data processing service was therefore to draw a flow graph which showed how these forms, or these packages of information, were created in one part of the organisation, and how they were sent on from workstation to workstation or from person to person, and how finally the information ended up in data bases which were more or less longlived. For the purpose of a systems designer, and for the purpose of dialogue with the end users, it was very convenient to use an *ad hoc* graphical language to describe the flow paths. We used it for specification work. We also implemented a tool whereby we could input such a flow graph into the computer, and interpret it in prototype style in order to show what the intended new services would be like when implemented on personal computers. After this prototype had been debugged in cooperation with the users, it could be rapidly transferred to everyday use.

The software for supporting the information flow is also an example of another principle that we inherited from our previous AI activities. In AI research projects there are a large number of cases where people write special purpose tools which operate on a special purpose language. They have identified some aspect of the application domain or some aspect of a technical system which lends itself to a concise description in a *special purpose language*. Then they implement an interpreter or a compiler for that language. Indeed LISP has been characterised as a very high level implementation language. It is a very convenient tool if you want to implement a number of such special purpose languages, and enable them to work nicely together. We brought the same practice into the more mundane domain of office systems.

Another such tool, which we also found quite convenient, was dialogue software supporting *dialogue transition networks* (Hägglund 1980, Hägglund and Oskarsson 1975). You can think of them as a tool for writing adventure games. There seem to be quite a number of applications where the user needs to navigate in a dialogue space. Each point in the space, or each node in the dialogue transition network, consists of one interaction. In each node of the network, the user is presented with one printout, or one screenful from the computer. Also for each node the allowable inputs from the user were defined. The present node and the user input together determine the next node to be used in the dialogue.

This dialogue pattern re-emerged from time to time. Of course if the network is very simple you can implement it easily in any programming language and environment, but quite often we needed to have a fairly large number of such nodes, and a large space for the user to navigate in. Then it was convenient to have a tool where you could interactively build the network and interpret it. This brought several advantages, including the advantage of rapid prototyping. We would let the system designer and the end user sit together at the terminal. The end user could try his hand (or her hand) navigating in the dialogue network to get things done. If some aspect of the system seemed to be counterintuitive or difficult to understand, then the system designer, who was the other person at the terminal, could go in and very rapidly modify the network and let the user try again.

Yet another tool, and the last one which I will describe, was a tool for distribution of modules to subsystems (Sandewall *et al.* 1981). This need arose especially as an extension of the information flow service. In the organisation we looked at there were a number of workstations, and hence a number of users. There were also a number of separate services, each of which could well be described as an information flow. So we had a kind of a matrix structure for the software. Each user, or each user workstation, was affected by a number of the services, and each service affected several workstations.

Because of the 2-dimensional structure of the problem, we had a difference between how we wanted to cut the software at development time, and how we wanted to cut it at run time. At development time it was reasonable to develop each of these information flow services, one at a time. We could take a bird's eye view of how one particular kind of information package would flow through the organisation. At run time, however, we wanted instead to have the software which was relevant for one particular user in his or her workstation, or in his or her workspace in the central computer.

The appropriate tool for the development phase, therefore, was a *development environment* which contained one information flow model, including all the components for all the different users which were involved along its flow path. When the model had been debugged, we wanted to decompose it into the pieces which belonged to the individual workers along the path, and distribute those pieces to the end user environments of the respective participants. Conversely, since each end user environment needed contributions from several flow paths, it needed to receive contributions from several such development environments. This defined how the general purpose module distribution system should work. It should allow one to generate a contribution from one environment and send it to another environment where it could be nicely integrated into the right places.

In order to get that principle to work properly we needed to pick up yet one other key method from artificial intelligence software techniques. Namely, it was necessary to store data, and descriptions of data and procedures, in an integrated way in a data base. In traditional programming we are used to storing data and programs as text files, which means that manipulation of the procedures and manipulation of special purpose languages becomes fairly difficult.

What we do instead in the AI style software technology is to define a data base in which different kinds of formulae can be stored, and where executable procedures are just one kind of data.

This is also the kind of structure that we needed in these development systems or development environments. In them, we needed to manipulate forms descriptions, information flow descriptions, descriptions of end user environments, descriptions of the topology of the total data processing system that one was operating against, and so on. Based on these various special purpose descriptions, this environment must be able to extract the structures that could be sent out to the target workstations for run-time use.

A common idea in this list of key methods is that we used a system development environment, a kind of computer aided design system for software in order to support the various tools.

7.3   Some lessons from AI-based software technology

This section looks retrospectively at the experience that was gained during this period. What did the software look like? What were the bottlenecks? What were the difficulties which had to be overcome in later generations of the system? Secondly, I want to look over these methods from several ordinary points of view: the point of view of the programmer, the point of view of the end user and so on.

First, let us consider the software that was built. We thought while we were doing the work that we did a fairly decent job as programmers. Things were done according to the best prescriptions of structured programming, project management and so on. Yet after a number of years, of course, the accumulated set of software was fairly large and fairly difficult to extend and to work with. We went back to try to identify where the complexity arose. Which were the parts of the system that were difficult to develop and to maintain? For this analysis, we needed a model, shown in Figure 7.1, of the total structure of the system.

At the heart, we had the program execution system, which was a variety of the INTERLISP system. This provided the database in which descriptions and programs could be stored. There were various low level routines subordinate to it for executing services such as screen management, handling small text objects and so on. Immediately above the level of the program execution system, we had a number of information handling tools, such as forms management, command dialogue, configuration control, sending things to other environments and so on. Above it again, we had the level of application modelling tools such as the information flow tool that I described, and a few other, similar ones. Finally, on the highest level we had the specific services, so, for example, each particular use of the information flow model would be located on the top level.

In this software architecture, the complexity was quite clearly located on the level of information handling tools. The extent to which it was concentrated there was very surprising. The program execution system was given and did not offer any problems. The lowest level consisted of a few individual routines which could be written easily by any competent programmer, e.g. a competent undergraduate in computer science. Given a specification, he would go away and write the program and come back with it completed. The application modelling tools were also surprisingly simple. In the case of information flow, for example, the actual work of implementing the information flow model, given that the forms management system and the other underlying tools existed, was quite small

Figure 7.1: Software architecture for Linköping Office Information System

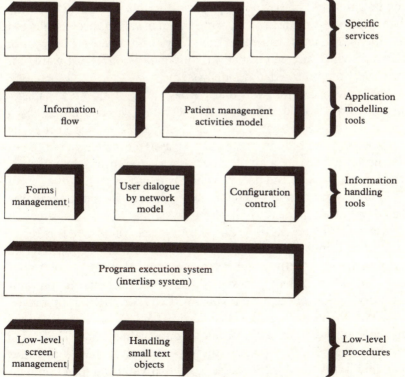

(Sandewall 1979). This has later been confirmed in the continuation of the project, where the idea of information flow has been transferred to software companies who built such information flow handlers on top of their forms management software and database software. Again the same story repeated: it was a small piece of software work. All the complexity arose on the level of the information handling tools. We therefore took as one of our goals in the research project to look over that level, as well as the total structure of the software, in order to reduce the complexity.

We now think the key to dealing with that complexity is to recognise an essential similarity between many of the office services. Essentially, in the office environment again and again we are building special purpose "mumble management systems" where *mumble* is a variable. We write telegram management systems that we call computer mail systems; appointment management systems that we call computer calendars; management systems for managing duties and promises which we call tickler files, and so on. The key idea in each of these is that you have a system which allows you to store data in the computer, and to put it in and bring it out piecewise. So another good term would be *systems for piecewise operations* on data – put the data in, move it around a bit and print it out in various projections and selections. In fact, this general framework also covers some types of software which are not usually thought of as office software, for example, computer aided design systems.

The first observation was that we have a lot of mumble management systems around. The second observation was that the essential similarity between many of those services are hidden by the terminology: not only by the names we assign to these systems, but also because there are a lot of unnecessary differences between their user interfaces. The end users repeatedly complained that the sets of operations were difficult to remember because "the same thing was called different names in different systems". This indicated an awareness and a perception from the end users that there was really "the same thing" in different software. So sometimes you have to write PRINT, sometimes TYPE, sometimes DISPLAY, and sometimes SHOW in order to see something on the terminal. If you want the information on a printer you say LIST or PRINT or maybe OUTPUT. Entering data is called ENTER or CREATE or NEW, or maybe you go into the editor even if you have new data. DELETE can be called REMOVE and I think several of us have sometimes searched frantically for the magic word that you need to get out of a piece of software. Should you say EXIT or STOP or QUIT or OK or BYE or whatever?

Clearly some kind of normalisation is needed here. Ideally, we should not have several separate systems in parallel to each other at all. Notice the reason that we have all the different names for the "same" operation is not that somebody intentionally created those alternative list of names in order to confuse the user. The reason is that we actually have parallel sets of software doing similar things. There is one whole program which does the operations in the first column of Figure 7.2, another program which does the operations in the second column, and so on. Instead of that software architecture, we would like to have a single piece of software which supports a matrix organisation, where the different operations with standardised names are listed in one dimension: PRINT, LIST, ENTER, EDIT and so on. The other dimension lists the various contexts or the various data environments. Ideally again, we would like to write the procedure for each of those operations just once.

In practice, that is not entirely possible. But there are going to be some differences (although perhaps marginal ones) between how you print out one entry in the mail system, and how you print out one entry in the address directory. The differences may depend on the structure of the data, but they may also depend on the character of the

Figure 7.2: An interactive command thesaurus

Application				
1	2	3	4	5
PRINT	TYPE	PRINT	DISPLAY	SHOW
LIST	PRINT	LIST	COPY	OUTPUT
ENTER	ENTER	CREATE	NEW	EDIT
EDIT	UPDATE	EDIT	CHANGE	EDIT
DELETE	REMOVE	DELETE	DELETE	DELETE
...	...	...	...	...
EXIT	STOP	END	QUIT	OK

application. So just having one procedure for each of the commands is not rich enough. What we can do instead is to say that for each context C and for each operation OP there should be one operator definition procedure. Often the operation definition procedure for similar contexts C or similar operations OP will be roughly the same.

In the worst case you have one procedure for each combination of context and operation. In practice we can rationalise it. In some cases several operations require a similar procedure and then we can form the abstraction from them. In some other cases the procedures associated with two different operations differ in some details. Then what you want to do is to write a joint procedure which covers the similarities, and also to have small attachments to those procedures which account for the differences between the operations.

Another thing about this repertoire of standardised operations is that many of them involve a traversal. In many cases the data structure is some kind of tree. Many of the standard operations make a scan over that tree and do something locally in each node. As an extension of the abstraction process, many of the operations can be characterised by a canned procedure which just traverses the tree, plus information which is specific to each operation. The add-on information specifies what to do in the leaf of a tree, what to do if the sub-tree you are trying to traverse does not exist and so on. For example, if you make a data access and you are trying to access a piece of information which does not exist, you will just give up. On the other hand, if you try to put the information into a part of the tree, and the place where you are trying to put it does not exist, then it should be created and inserted into the tree so that you can put your data there.

The general framework was therefore to identify those operations which had the character of tree traversal, and to form a joint abstraction for them. We then associated the general purpose tree traversal procedure with that abstraction. With the lower level nodes in the abstraction tree for operations we associated the detailed procedures which specify how to handle the leaf, and how to handle a missing daughter in the tree, and so on.

Using the design principles that I have now outlined, we were able to rewrite the editor level of the system. After a number of iterations over complex systems, we were able to build a compact system which served quite well in the office environment, and which implemented these key methods which we carried with us as our methodological baggage.

Clearly none of the services which I have described contains any particular intelligence. If we look back on the figure of the structure of the software (Figure 7.1), the logical place to put the kind of intelligence facilities that are used in expert systems and other AI systems is on the level of application modelling tools. Things like rule-based reasoning, and maybe also truth maintenance logically belong there. We therefore thought it was encouraging that what we did on this level was relatively simple and turned out to be easy to implement. That showed that in terms of the complexity constraints of the total system, there was a lot of available "space" there. After we had brought everything into good order up to the level of this information management system, we were able to provide the standard office services very easily. We felt we had plenty of room for adding more intelligence.

This observation provides the key to the strategy I want to propose for introducing AI techniques and expert system techniques into conventional data processing. If you feel that today's expert system packages do significant things for you, if they are worth their price and if they are worth the effort of introducing them, then fine, go ahead. If it is instead your feeling that the expert system technology is not yet mature for the applications you have in mind, then maybe you wish to wait a few years before putting it into wider application in your own operations. At the same time you may be looking for ways of positioning yourself, and positioning your software so that those same AI techniques can be introduced easily and flexibly when the time arrives.

The style of software architecture which is described in this paper may then fit in nicely. It has a lot of merit in itself, so it is worth doing quite apart from whether you are going to use AI later on. But, at the same time, it puts you in a much better position for introducing AI techniques later on, than if you pursue the traditional COBOL-based or similar software engineering methods.

7.4 New approaches to systems development

In the final part of this essay I want to review the proposed software strategy from a number of additional viewpoints. After all, if we introduce a new software strategy we must know what we are doing. We must know how it affects everything else that is important in the operation of data processing.

Software engineering. Let us first consider how this strategy can be seen from a general engineering viewpoint. The term "software engineering" has been introduced in order to suggest similarities with other branches of engineering, and to suggest that this is a branch of engineering (which is not entirely obvious to other engineers). It has also been introduced in order to encourage us to borrow ideas and principles from other branches of engineering.

One of the standard engineering methods, which is very often recommended, is modularity. It is considered to be a good idea to recognise recurrent phenomena and recurrent needs, and to package solutions for those needs into a standardised format. Usually modularity has been identified with the use of subroutines or other similar things, which means that modules are components which can be assembled into larger systems. Now I claim that, in engineering in general, this is not the only important aspect of modularity.

One example of subroutine style modularity is shown in Figure 7.3. Here we have built an aeroplane from standardised components. Of course, the components do not always fit the purpose precisely, but at least something has been built.

Figure 7.4 shows an example of the other kind of modularity, which is sometimes referred to as a *universal tool*. Here the designer of this tool has identified one class of applications in the workshop and has built a tool which supports whatever is common

Figure 7.3: Subroutine style modularity

Figure 7.4: A universal tool

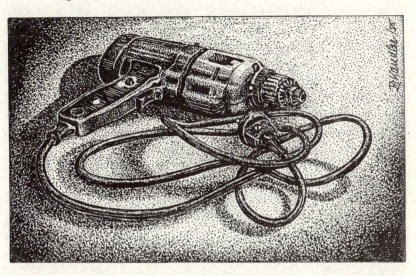

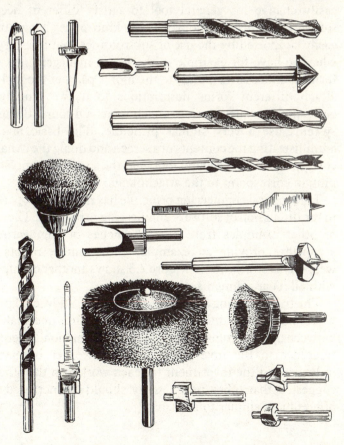

for that whole class of application. The common tool here, the universal tool, contains an electric motor, and a cord, and controls so that you can turn on and turn off the motor. A wide flexibility is guaranteed because we can make various attachments to the chuck: a drill, a polisher, and so on. Almost everything that is significant for the use of this tool is concentrated in the exchangeable parts. On the other hand consider the total cost of the system: the major cost is in that part which is common. Another thing which is very important is that there must be a device (in this case the chuck) which allows you to easily and safely swop the changeable parts.

What has been shown here is *not* the same kind of modularity as we had in the previous case: it is not the modularity which arises because you have standardised components. Component modularity also arises because we may have used, e.g., a standard, off-the-shelf cord in the production of the basic tool. But the significant modularity, for the purpose of this discussion, is the modularity which is seen by the owner of the tool: the end user who is able to easily change his general tool to satisfy different needs. In the software engineering domain, this kind of exchangeability is not easily supported by the use of sub-routines, but it is very similar to what we have for example in the forms management system. The forms handler corresponds to the motor parts of the tool, and as we attach different forms descriptions to it, we plug in whatever corresponds to these various attachments. Of course the spreadsheets systems use a very similar principle. The basic machinery for administrating the contents of a screen and doing the dynamic update corresponds to the general tool, and the so-called templates that you plug in correspond to the attachments.

This general engineering principle has not been properly observed in the discussion of software engineering principles. There are plenty of other examples from other branches of engineering. Fighter aeroplanes provide an example, with bombs, robots and other weapons as attachments. Figure 7.5 shows another example, a tractor with all its attachments.

The tractor analogy is interesting from an additional point of view when we discuss office systems. Quite often one makes parallels between office automation and factory automation. There is frequent reference to the investment for each worker in manufacturing industry and the investment for each worker in the office, and it is suggested that office productivity should be increased by making offices more similar to industry.

This trend is accentuated by the choice of terms such as "office worker" and maybe also "knowledge worker". The use of the term "worker" may be because people wish to apply the methods of Taylor, or may be due to socialist romanticism, but in either case I believe the analogy with industry is not the only relevant one. There have been objections to whether industrialisation of offices is a desirable development, and fears have been voiced that work in the office could become as boring as work in manufacturing industry is often thought to be.

There is, however, another branch of society which has an even larger investment per worker, namely, agriculture. Certainly in farming we don't have the scenario of very routine work that is usually encountered along the assembly line. The individual farmer understands very well the domain that he is working in: the growing

Figure 7.5: Another universal tool

of the crops, the effects of the weather, and so on. At the same time he has at his disposal a number of very powerful tools whereby he can fairly independently manage his work.

I therefore want to suggest that we should not look for the "office worker" in the future, but rather for the "information farmer": the individual person who does independent work using very powerful tools. The tractor that the farmer has as one of his tools would then correspond to general purpose software tools into which the end user can plug his particular templates or descriptions of the job to be done.

Data processing. Although we have examined the issues of general engineering principles and the view of the end user, it is also necessary to say something about the data processing perspective.

We have seen how some data processing services could be immersed into a general purpose editor. We could also see, in the course of our research project, how various other data processing services in the office could be nicely characterised by special purpose languages, for example, the information flow application. But what about the remaining services? Will these two techniques cover every kind of data processing in the office?

There is a very interesting paper by Boehm who organised students to write and implement a few medium size office applications (Boehm 1980). They measured how much time was spent on different activities, and how many lines of software were generated for various activities. The interesting result was that the "job at hand" was served by only 2%–3% of the number of lines of code. The algorithm for doing the work that was the purpose of the program was a small fraction of the code! Everything else was for things like general housekeeping of the data, error handling, describing the data that needed to be operated on, checking for incorrect input from the user, supporting the user with a convenient data entry language, and so on and so on.

In the terms that I introduced earlier, I would say that 98% of that special purpose program did information management and only 2% did the things which were application specific. So from this point of view maybe text editors, forms handlers and so on are just the limiting cases of a general principle, namely the cases where the algorithm is 0% rather than 2%. This suggests that the right way to organise this kind of software should be to build the information management system first, in order to cover 95 or 100% of the task.

When an algorithm needs to be added, it should be possible to plug it in. A good information management system should be able to receive "plug in" procedures which account for the things that distinguish different applications. This of course confirms again the idea of using software with "plug in" modularity.

Language design. Another perspective from which to look at this software technology is from the perspective of programming languages. In the literature, there have been a very large number of papers about how to design good programming languages. These papers reflect several different schools. In particular there is the ALGOL-like school, the school which started in FORTRAN and ALGOL which has later on generated PASCAL, Ada and so on. There is another school of thought which is represented by incremental languages such as LISP, APL, MUMPS, to some extent BASIC, and more recently PROLOG.

Almost all this normative or even moralistic literature about what is a good programming language comes from the first of these two schools. We may speculate why that is so. With respect to LISP, which has been used in AI projects, my explanation is that the users have often been graduate students who were interested in the various aspects of the LISP system they were using as a tool. But the research leaders have often discouraged the study of the LISP as such, because they saw a danger of losing sight of the main issue, which was the design of AI. Therefore, over the years, there has been pressure to discourage too much delving about in the tools. In the area of classical programming languages, there has not been the same kind of restraint, because there the programming language was *the* topic of interest and therefore was considered to be the appropriate thing to write about.

There is therefore a philosophical position about programming languages which is quite widespread in actual work but which has not been as often articulated in the literature. Figure 7.6 illustrates one important difference between the two schools of thought. In the LISP environment, the key idea when you build a system is to first build a data base where you can store expressions. These expressions can be, e.g., expressions in logic, or expressions which describe forms in a forms management system, or descriptions of data corresponding to the Data Divison in a COBOL program. But they can also be procedures, as another special case.

When we receive complaints about the bad, parenthesis-oriented syntax of LISP programs, compared to the syntax in, for example, ALGOL with all its syntactic sugar, the explanation for the difference is that the notation used in LISP is not specially designed for procedures. It is more general than that. We have a basis which is able to store expressions in a data base. On top of that, the data base is used for storing procedure definitions, application modules, software management information, application data, and so on and so on in an integrated way.

In the classical school, the programming language performs both the service of "programming in the small" and "programming in the large". That is, it allows us to express the contents of procedures, conditional statements, statement sequencing, loops and so on, and it also allows us to define block structure and other global structures. On top of that there will be module management. In sophisticated systems there may be program generators, and there may be a command system for the operating system or a programmable shell.

In the conventional programming language architecture there are these different layers which are stacked on top of each other. In the LISP environment, on the other hand, the lowest level, the expression level, is intended only to correspond to the local aspects of the programming language – "programming in the small". Everything else is programmed in that language, in an integrated way. I think it is important to keep this correspondence in mind when you compare

Figure 7.6: **Programming language and systems**

Conventional	LISP style
Programmable shell	Data base containing application models and software management information
Program generators	
Programming-in-the-large	
Global programming language constructs (e.g. block structure)	
Programming-in-the-small	Expressions in a simple procedural or functional programming language

programming languages, for example, LISP to PASCAL or LISP to Ada. Don't compare all of kernal LISP with all of Ada because then you are comparing structures that were intended for different ranges of notational service.

Development methodology. Yet another perspective to take on this software technology is with respect to the stages of development of a piece of software. We are used to thinking about two stages – specification and implementation. In the debate about rapid proto- typing, which is yet another novel technology, we sometimes encounter the question of where prototyping fits in. Is prototyping a part of the specification phase or is it a part of the implementation phase? It is sobering, in such a discussion, to remember that the distinction between specification and implementation has not been there always.

If we go back to the early days of data processing: the 50's and early 60's before procedural languages were in widespread use, we would rather have used the stages shown in Figure 7.7. There was problem analysis, followed by flow charting where flow charting was of course done "off line" and not in direct connection with a computer. Instead it involved the preparation of drawings which could be used as a specification for the person who wrote the machine code.

These three stages therefore do not correspond directly to the stages of specification and implementation. Some of what we do now in specification would have been done in flow charting earlier,

Figure 7.7. Development methodologies

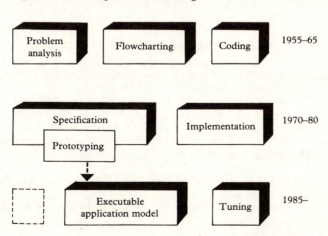

but flow charting also overlaps with what we now do in implementation in a procedural language.

If such a switch has occurred before, it may occur again. My proposal is that the methodology from now on is likely to be increasingly one where we have an initial thinking phase and a phase of dialogue with users. Then there is a phase where we develop an *executable application model* in the computer: something which runs in the computer aided design system for software. For example, in the case of information flow modelling, this stage would be the stage where the information flow model is built up in the computer and tested in co-operation with the users. When this executable application model has been finished and judged satisfactory, there is either transition to practical use, using automatic software tools, or a short stage of manual tuning in order to speed up the system. But the essential design work would then be done in the software design system or design environment, by building and checking the executable application model.

7.5　Conclusions

To summarise very briefly the message of this chapter is that editors or information management systems are a key element in software architecture. They are important as end user tools. They are also important as parts of system development environments, because during system development we are going to edit or modify the application model continuously. Every step towards extended use of such information management systems in practical data processing operations today is valuable in itself, but it also paves the road for increased use of AI technology over the years to come.

References and suggestions for further reading

Boehm, B.W. (1980). Developing small-scale application software products: some experimental results. In *Information Processing 80*, ed. S.H. Lavington, pp. 321 – 326. Amsterdam: North Holland.

Hägglund, S. (1980). Contributions to the development of methods and tools for interactive design of applications software. Ph.D. thesis, Department of Computer and Information Science. Linköping, Sweden: Linköping University.

Hägglund, S. and Oskarsson, Ö. (1975). IDECS2 User's Guide. Report DLU 75/3, Datalogilaboratoriet, Uppsala, Sweden: Uppsala University.

Sandewall, E. (1979). A description language and pilot-system executive for *information transport systems*. In *Proc. Fifth International Conference on Very Large Data Bases*. Rio de Janeiro.

Sandewall, E. (1982). Unified dialogue management in the carousel System. In

Proc. ACM Conference on Principles of Programming Languages. Albuquerque, NM.

Sandewall, E. Strömberg, C. and Sörenson, H. (1981). Software architecture based on communicating residential environments. In *Proc. Fifth International Conference on Software Engineering.* San Diego.

Strömfors, O. and Jonesjö, L (1981). The implementation and experiences of a structure-oriented text editor. In *Proc. ACM SIGPLAN/SIGOA Symposium on Text Manipulation. SIGPLAN Notices*, Vol. 16, No. 6.

8 AI in business

IAN BENSON

8.1 Introduction

The previous chapters have described major research directions in artificial intelligence and computer science. In this essay we will look at the process of diffusion of the new technology into everyday use, and in particular at its implications for systems development and information systems research.

The essay begins with a review of the state of the art achieved in research laboratories and describes some of the special purpose hardware and software tools which emerged from them in the early eighties. It continues with an examination of the factors affecting the takeup of these techniques, with case studies of the implementation of knowledge based systems at British Airways, Unilever and Cognitive Systems. The final section looks at the cultural revolution in system development methods and highlights the critical role of modern information systems in determining options for work organisation and performance.

8.2 The state of the art in intelligent systems

The previous essays have given several examples of intelligent systems. In order to assess the overall state of the art, their authors were asked by Karen Sparck Jones at the Cambridge conference to comment on the construction of two imaginary systems. One was a fetch-and-carry robot and the other a personal information assistant (PIA).

The contributors were asked whether there were any building blocks or modules (using this in rather a loose sense, not necessarily bits of code) which could be pulled in from different sources, from places where they have already been tried out, to put together and build slightly more powerful or more comprehensive systems than already exist. For example, was it possible to combine the kind of rule induction that has been done in some expert systems or robotics contexts with say a semantic grammar in order to enable user modelling of an interface to an operating system? The second question was what global principles or concepts might be applied to motivate the overall system design. For example, is enough known to suggest that it is the right thing to do to treat any system you want to build as a planning system?

The two imaginary systems were chosen because unintelligent versions of both already exist. There are very simple tracked industrial lifting devices and personal information assistants which carry out selective dissemination of bibliographic information. In both areas more intelligence would be very useful. It is possible to imagine a general purpose store assistant controlled by natural language. This would operate like a person who picked up boxes, put them on to a trolley, trundled them around and so on. Similarly, a general purpose document handler which could deal with electronic mail, arrange meetings, answer letters and so on, carrying out several of the functions of secretarial assistants, would be very useful.

Such systems would need a range of capabilities. It would be necessary to integrate features found at present in one-off experimental systems. It was also clear that there were a wide range of possible options from the trivial to the very glossy. Participants were asked to present their views on where we stand within this range today.

Personal Information Assistant. It was generally agreed that the personal information assistant was an easier task to implement than the fetch-and-carry robot. The PIA was imagined to run on a home computer hooked into a telephone network communicating with similar machines. In this kind of situation the capability of the machine is a function of the state of the art in natural language processing alone. This depends on delimiting the domain of discourse so that a fairly thorough analysis can be done about the domain and the language used to talk about it. Today natural language processing systems operate pretty well in narrow domains, like ordering groceries from a grocery shop. There is a long way to go before a PIA could read general messages coming from other people, and sort them according to some set of real semantic categories as opposed to doing keyword look-up.

Fetch-and-carry robot. Prototype fetch-and-carry robots are under construction in a number of centres. At SRI "Son of Shakey" is currently being built to integrate reasoning, perception and natural language communication to enable people to direct a robot using natural language. At the Naval Ocean Systems Center in San Diego there is a mail delivering robot which comes down the hall ringing a bell.

The key limiting factors are perception and the ability to model the robot's environment in a predictable fashion. What this means is typically the need to strictly limit the number of objects, and easily distinguish one from another, perhaps using controlled lighting, special sensors, ultrasonic detectors, etc. In some cases, it is possible to recognise surfaces based on computations that are performed on the signals that are returned.

A first difficulty is concerned with the processing power needed to analyse the sensor images. With present technology up to 15 minutes is required to analyse a single picture. For real-time processing up to 30 pictures a second would need to be analysed.

Once the robot moves outside a strictly controlled environment the predictability of the behaviour of the other agents becomes a major factor. As long as there are a fixed range of possibilities that the robot needs to consider, a computer can do a pretty good job at exploring out game trees. The performance of computer chess players demonstrates this capability.

Jean-Claude Latombe has adopted an approach to ensuring co-operation of multiple agents, whether human or robot, by defining some "social" laws to enable the agents to co-operate or cohabit. There is an analogy here with the Rules of the Road. It is necessary to define a protocol for how a car should behave in relation to other cars when it reaches a crossroads. The same kind of code needs to be developed for a set of robots interacting. As with cars, these codes will not necessarily prevent accidents from happening.

At present assumptions about the behaviour of other agents can be extremely crude and are often hard-wired into the robot. For instance, in John Cobb's case, there was an assumption about obstacles in the environment not moving over time. Clearly the designer of such a robot cannot anticipate in great detail every possible situation a robot might encounter. The best that might be done is to develop some reasonable safeguards. For example, objects might be classified so that by identifying which class an object belongs to it is possible for the computer to predict how it might act. For example, human beings move somewhat unpredictably, other objects move somewhat predictably, etc. What is needed is a general approach to building systems of this sort which enables the easy isolation of such assumptions as the system grows, so that more capabilities can be added.

The problem of abstracting assumptions about the environment made in robotic systems is an example of a general problem that AI lags behind other parts of computer science in its system development methods. For example, a lot of work can go into defining the knowledge that a system is supposed to contain in a particular application, but the knowledge representation adopted is not readily transferable to a second application system. It is possible to imagine, say, a system which knew about cups and saucers and material objects in the world but this knowledge would not be in the form today that could make it accessible to many different applications which needed that knowledge for different purposes. A first attempt at such an integrative project at SRI was the "commonsense summer" project in 1984 which attempted to formalise commonsense knowledge in a way that would be usable both for robotics applications and for natural language applications.

A solution to the problem of multiple agents interacting will ultimately require advances here, and in *planning, communication, simulation* and *learning*. At present, reasonable *plans* can only be generated for small closed worlds where the states are certain and the operators are deterministic. *Communication* is a planning process where there are lots of states that are fuzzy and hard to bound and there are no really good integrated notions about how integrate planning, sensing and communication to make an overall system that is capable of reasoning.

Simulation is a third area that can benefit from advances in the state of the art since this is what will be used to predict what is likely to happen on the basis of some action that might be taken. For example, if a fetch-and-carry robot is going to carry groceries (and manipulate eggs and cans, say) it ought to have some knowledge about naive, or not so naive, physics.

Learning is the most speculative of all four research areas. The goal here is not only to solve the learning problem but to state it, and this cannot be done until there are better ideas of what the end result is to be of the learning process. Thus the focus of learning research lies in knowledge representation.

Finally the problem of multi-agent modelling may also require a significant paradigm shift in the way in which interactions are modelled. The "command" paradigm is needed for single agent systems, since the object is to construct machines whose behaviour is controlled. The last opportunity to shape their behaviour should not be the point at which the machine is switched on. Other paradigms have become useful at lower levels, in perception for instance. Here, the pandemonium model has been proposed of autonomous neurons competing to get the attention of a neuron at a higher level than them all. Similar paradigms will probably become more and more important in integrating information from different sources and in multi-agent planning.

8.3   New software tools

Prompted by the success of some of the late seventies intelligent systems, such as PROSPECTOR, at first a trickle and then a flood of new software tools began to appear. Figure 8.1 shows some of the earlier releases.

The software fell into three classes: symbolic language interpreters, and associated programming environments, knowledge based system shells, and natural language database front-ends.

Languages for symbolic computation. The LISP families of researchers at the major US universities each spawned their own programming environment and for some of these special purpose hardware, or LISP machines, were built. On the west coast of America, INTERLISP and the Xerox D machines (Dorado, Dolphin, Dandelion) came out of Xerox's Palo Alto Research Center. In the east, MIT's MACLISP gave rise to LISP machines and SYMBO-LICS computers with their version named ZETA-LISP, a name now also adopted by MIT. A widely used dialect, FRANZLISP, was produced by the University of California at Berkeley, and runs on DEC VAX's under Unix.

The attempts at LISP standardisation are focused on COMMON LISP, for which implementations began to appear on the IBM PC in the mid-eighties. At a conference convened by the US Department of Defence in 1984 to discuss the future of the LISP, it was stated that the DoD would support COMMON LISP, which is close to ZETA-LISP.

PROLOG was first implemented in 1972 by Alan Colmerauer's team in Marseilles, as a tool for natural language processing research. A team of Hungarian scientists implemented the language in 1975 and have used it since then as the basis for practical applications, sometimes with embedded FORTRAN routines. Widespread use of PROLOG in the European academic community followed the implementation in 1977 of the DEC-10 version of the language by David Warren at Edinburgh University. A version of the language for personal computers, MicroPROLOG was developed in 1980.

Today, major manufacturers are investigating PROLOG machines, both sequential and parallel. For example, IBM, Burroughs, MCC, and Schlumberger. The Mitsubishi PSI machine is likely to be available commercially in late 1985, having been

Figure 8.1: Contemporary developments in AI software tools

		RAMIS English
		LOGOS
		MPROLOG
		LOGICIAN
		AIKIT
		KIDS
		KBMS
	REVEAL	NLI
	SILL	IKBM
	T	PROTEUS
	KES	EASE
	DUCK	ARBY
	MICRO-PROLOG	K-BASE
	APES	PLUME
INTERLISP	OPS83	M1
ZETALISP	SAGE	S1
PROLOG	KS-300	GCLISP
OPS	AL/X	OPS5e
KAS	MRS	LISP/VM
INTELLECT	KEE	SRL +
EMYCIN	LOOPS	ART

1980 1985

demonstrated at the 1984 FGCS Tokyo conference. Attention is now turning to the development of PROLOG programming environments for sequential and parallel machines and to application areas such as commercial data processing and a wider range of expert systems.

A third class of symbolic language interpreters has emerged from the object-oriented programming school. In contrast to the functional, and declarative views of programming represented by LISP and PROLOG, object-oriented programming regards the computing process as the development of a system through sequences of changing states, the system consisting of objects. The Simula languages were the first to present this perspective (Dahl and Nygaard 1975, Dahl, Myhrlang and Nygaard 1968) with Smalltalk an important later example (Goldberg and Robson 1983). Facilities for object-oriented programming have been introduced in LISP (Flavors in ZETA-LISP and LOOPS in INTERLISP).

Knowledge based system shells. In the last few years a variety of commercial IKBS shells have begun to appear. Although much less sophisticated than the shiny systems implemented on the LISP machines they captured the essence of the induction methods used there. Thus EMYCIN and PROSPECTOR spawned AL/X, SAGE, KS-300 and M1. Out of CMU came OPS and its family of dialects OPS83 and OPS5e, etc.

Daniel Sagalowicz, of Teknowledge, has described the application of these shells as being appropriate to three kinds of problem. The first area is *structured selection.* That is, problems of diagnosis or choice, in which the number of possible answers is fairly limited but the number of possible questions is very large. In diagnosis, there are many things which can happen. These are problems with a class of solutions which are traditionally implemented by backward chaining.

The second class of problems is *configuration planning.* Here the problem is exactly the reverse. In configuration planning, the constraints are known, and although there may only be a limited number of them, the world of possible solutions is very large. For example, the world of possible DEC VAX configurations is very large. These problems are essentially forward chaining types of problem.

The third type of problem which has been looked at is *signal interpretation.* Interpreting a seismic signal, an X-ray, or an

ECG. Solutions have some aspects of backward chaining and some aspects of forward chaining.

Today, the best understood technology is the first class – the backward chaining problems. Then come forward chaining problems, with the third class being the most difficult (Winston and Prendergast 1984).

In the medium term there will be an increasing number of vendors who will produce intelligent instruments, which combine data collection and analysis, while other vendors will provide "generic" expert systems. These are expert systems which have some knowledge common to a large group of people. For example, expert systems in the financial market, in the credit market, or the insurance market. Generic problems will be adapted to each particular case but the vendors will sell a generic expert system.

An early example of such a company is provided by Syntelligence. They are developing a "corporate lending adviser" aimed at insurance underwriting and other financial institutions. The program assists the banker by requesting information, largely in accordance with the industrial classification of his or her prospective client. The system leads the banker through an electronic worksheet, which can be filled in in any order. At any point the system can provide information on how the loan is doing. In the real world the cost of gathering extra information may not be worth the reduction in risk it would apply. The system therefore also indicates sensitivities, where the range of risk is high, with prompts such as: "Two years of balance sheet data would help in narrowing the risk".

The objective of the system is to ensure that the loan officer takes into account all relevant factors and weighs them properly and picks up the risks he is taking. It enables the bank to impose consistency on its service.

In the longer term, Teknowledge believe that a market will emerge for expert-to-expert, or company-to-company, knowledge to be exchanged. Around the end of the decade, there will be expert systems which aim at attacking the home computer market. Here there will be complete frozen expert systems with inbuilt knowledge. How that market might develop is extremely unclear.

Natural language processing. The third class of AI based software are tools for building natural languages interfaces.

There are a broad range of natural language tools available which enable a systems designer to build a natural language interface to a database. If the database contains a single file, and the user knows its contents, then it is possible to interrogate the file without needing to know the syntax of the query language or the names of the fields. Such systems range from INTELLECT which runs on IBM mainframes and costs around $70,000 to packages such as CLOUT which run on a PC for under a thousand dollars.

The operation of such a system would follow a straightforward pattern. For instance, with a database containing information on salesmen the user might ask questions such as "Which of my sales people in the north-east region earned over forty thousand dollars?" or, "Rank their last year's sales in descending order by region". The key here is that the user knows that the database contains information giving the region a sales person works in, their salary, sales, etc.

8.4   IKBS in industry

In this section we will look at the way in which expert system techniques have been introduced at British Airways and Unilever, and Cognitive Systems' assessment of the strengths and limitations of contemporary natural language processing systems.

British Airways. British Airways is a sophisticated computer user, with well developed decision support systems. Although BA sees substantial long term potential in the new techniques there are still significant problems of scale and system integration to be solved. Its strategy for implementing IKBS has focussed on identifying the classes of decision support needed by different groups of staff, paying particular attention to areas within which there are wide differences in performance. Criteria have been proposed for identifying these groups, and the construction of a prototype knowledge based system is currently under way in the rostering area.

British Airways already has models, computer programs, that will help forecast, for example, the impact of changing flight timetables on expected punctuality, or the number of people that might have to be employed at an airport and the best methods of rostering them, or when they should report, or how many there should be in each gang, or the number of backups needed on a shuttle, and so on. BA takes in £5m a day in forty currencies and decision support systems assist in deciding where to place it overnight. There are already three or four hundred man years of programming invested in these systems.

Looking around the airline, prominent experts are precisely those people who already have these well developed decision support systems. They are typically in staff functions, helping other people to make decisions. It is this distinction which has been the basis of BA's implementation strategy for knowledge based systems.

Decision support work is now classified into two groups. There is that work which refers to a small group of experts. It is not the intention to make their knowledge widely available. The objective is to improve their own knowledge – to ensure that the sum of man and machine is more effective than man alone can be. These are the people who have been the traditional subjects for operational research (OR) groups and have been well served by them. For this reason they are not felt to be good candidates for an initial knowledge based system development.

The second area for decision support occurs where there is a large group of people where some are noticeably better than the average. The objective would be to give the larger group access to the knowledge of the experts. A second criterion is that this must be in an area which has not got very well developed traditional OR or mathematically based decision support. It is much more difficult to produce something effective within a year or eighteen months if you are trying at the same time to displace already well established tools.

With those criteria in mind BA have selected the rostering area as being appropriate for the initial development of a knowledge based system. Rostering decisions are made throughout the world yet there are only a small group of people who are very good at it. As these are Operational Research professionals they are good candidates to be knowledge engineers. It is hoped that, by having domain experts and knowledge engineers as almost the same group, rostering staff scattered throughout the world will be significantly aided by the new system.

In the longer term one of the major advantages of these new techniques will be derived from the way in which they enable rules to be abstracted from programs. For example, the crew scheduling program, in which the rules for rostering crew are embedded, has been reimplemented five or six times in the last ten years in four languages on five different machines. The ability to separate out rules and make them explicit will significantly ease the process of renovation.

For this to happen, however, there are still significant problems of scale and system integration to be solved. Simple PC based systems will not be sufficient. For example, a fares system would have to be integrated into existing networks and be able to cope with significant transaction volumes. BA's fares system handles two and a half thousand transactions an hour, and has more than a million fares.

The solution to these problems of scale can only come from a merging of the concerns of the traditionally distinct AI and EDP communities.

Unilever. Unilever, the 15th largest company in the world, has a radically different organisational structure from the centralised British Airways. It consists of more than 500 operating companies in seventy-five countries with a significant degree of local autonomy. The companies trade as suppliers to the grocery business, selling margarine, soap, detergent, shampoo, frozen products, ice cream etc.

Unilever has several characteristics which indicate that AI technology has a potentially great value. Firstly it operates in both developed and less developed countries, and employs staff with a wide range of skill levels. Secondly although operations and management are decentralised, there are strong central activities in things like research and engineering, and functional activities such as marketing, economics and personnel. Thirdly a major problem faced by the company is making this central expertise available in parts of the world where communications are difficult and skill levels are very low.

At present these internal information flows are handled by people visiting, telephone calls and written reports. These are not particularly effective techniques for providing advice, assistance and problem solving at a local level. AI techniques are seen as a useful supplement to these traditional methods.

Unilever's approach to AI started around 1980 within its Central R & D facility. They developed inhouse systems for their own use, which classified research findings, and they carried out experiments with the use of these systems by scientists.

In 1983 Unilever began moving some of these systems outside the research environment. The first area to be tackled was the technical side of the business in individual companies. Opportunities were sought for using rule based expert systems in areas such as machinery maintenance, packaging, local product development, quality control and microbiology.

Machinery is a big part of Unilever's activity around the world. The ability to maintain it with low skill levels is quite important.

Packaging of consumer goods is another key activity. Since the availability of packaging materials differs in one part of the world from another, there is a need to identify equivalent materials and ascertain how they might be used. Often product development is carried out locally, and knowledge based systems developed in the research environment can reduce the amount of wasted development activity in the field. In particular quality control can be ordered by incorporating important rules to set up families of tests and interpret their results. This is particularly true with respect to establishing the microbiological safety of food products. Here again, there are fairly low level skills available in this area within local operating companies and knowledge based systems offer an opportunity to build up this expertise.

By the mid-eighties Unilever will have moved beyond technical systems into commerce, finance and marketing. Similar AI techniques offer opportunities for organising and representing knowledge in commercial areas such as foreign exchange dealing and financing. In marketing, several possibilities have been found ranging from the provision of information on the corporate philosophy of how to market, to the use of knowledge based systems as tools to help sell.

Three key criteria have influenced the diffusion of AI and knowledge system techniques in the company.

Portability. The early work on AI had been carried out on specialist machines such as DEC's VAX. This inhibited the transfer of systems around the world and the later stages have therefore concentrated on a development of systems running on the IBM PC.

Expert system shells. A key limitation on the scale of experiment is the availability of skilled manpower. It was therefore important that users could carry out their own development at the earliest possible stage. To aid this process relatively simple and small domains were selected and two expert systems shells evaluated which enabled users to begin to develop workable systems with only a few days' training.

Security. Unilever see security and confidentiality as a major issue in determining an appropriate division of labour between users and vendors. Since the systems contain competitive information Unilever does not look to external vendors to supply complete packages but rather to develop shells. Shells which have been evaluated include SYNICS, EXPERT, PROSPECTOR, SAVOIR, and EXPERTISE.

Unilever's experience has pointed to the need for more work in several directions. Firstly, there is a need to provide better tools for knowledge engineering to be used by experts on a do-it-yourself basis. Secondly, the man–machine interface should be significantly enhanced by linking expert systems to animated graphics and video. This would be particularly useful, for example, in microbiology to display cultures, or in machine maintenance to show pictures of parts.

Thirdly, it was found that the performance of inference systems does not degrade gracefully as the system moves outside its domain of reference. In addition, systems like PROSPECTOR may require enhancement to account properly for situations of low probability but high risk.

Fourthly Unilever is concerned with the problem of developing systems which can accept and output natural languages other than English. It is certainly not sufficient to assume that the users of ubiquitous systems will have English either as a native tongue, or even as a language at all.

Cognitive Systems. Cognitive Systems is an AI based start-up company, concerned with implementing knowledge based systems in industry. They have a background in the "Yale" school of natural language processing, and this informed their assessment of the strengths and limitations of existing techniques.

Contemporary tools are restricted to the construction of natural language systems which interface with a single file, and operate where the user is aware of its contents. Databases with this characteristic are basically used by middle managers. Somebody like a personnel manager who essentially deals with a single file of information.

For other levels in the company, the situation is not so straightforward. If, for example, the president of a company needs access to his accounting system, then the data he requires may be spread amongst several information systems covering, say, receivables, payables, inventories, general ledger, etc. The problem is that the way that information has been accessed in the past is through a series of regular reports – daily, weekly or monthly. It is possible to collate collate this information instantaneously using 4th Generation computer languages. They can provide some flexibility, but with all the attendant problems of non-natural language systems.

The kind of dialogue that the executive would like to have would be the ability to ask very simple questions such as

"How many executive desks did we ship to Jersey Supply today?" Then he wants to ask a following question, "How about this week?" The problem is that the information needed to answer these two questions comes from entirely different files. In fact even entirely different areas of the company. "How about in the last week?" is different from either of the other two and "How many ought to be shipped this week?" might turn out to be in the same file as "How about this week"? The ability to make this type of mapping is required for the solution to the executive's problem. A simple interface that only allows you to retrieve specific fields of information does not solve this problem.

For AI techniques to have a significant impact in the commercial world, implementers will have to resolve this kind of system integration problem. For example, the system may have to interface with several query languages, and perhaps enhance them. It may be that linking information is absent from fragments of files and so specific information will have to be generated automatically for the AI system or entered by a database manager.

Other real world constraints also apply. The database manager may be unable to spend more than a day learning how to carry out this new function. The time spent on the nightly update that produces the new information required by the AI system cannot exceed the amount of free time available in the overnight computer job queue, etc. The limitation then is that AI techniques need to be brought in alongside traditional data processing skills in order to provide solutions that are needed on a large scale to problems in the commercial world.

8.5   The revolution in systems development

The resolution of these problems will involve not only a change in the technical base of the industry, as dramatic in its way as the move from electro-mechanical to electronic calculating machines, but also a cultural revolution in the way that systems are constructed, and the respective roles of users, developers and vendors.

The presentations at the Cambridge conference of the objectives of the Japanese Fifth Generation Project indicated the ways in which the technical base is set to change. Driven by the continuing increase in circuit density obtainable in VLSI technology, their project aims to deliver by early in the next decade Super PCs with:

▶ 10 million instructions per second cycle time
▶ 4 megabyte main memory (using 4 megabit RAM available at the end of the eighties)
▶ Colour CRT with 1,000 × 1,000 pixel resolution. This has already been demonstrated by Sony who anticipate prototype CRTs with 2,000 × 2,000 resolution by the end of the eighties
▶ Electronic disks with 100 megabytes of memory
▶ Interfaces to high speed local area networks.

The Japanese intend the whole machine to cost less than a family car, of the order of $3,500 per annum. At their Tokyo conference in late 1984 they unveiled the Personal Sequential Inference (PSI) machine on which the Super PCs will be based. Their vision of how this extra computing power will be used is shown in Figure 8.2. The Knowledge Information Processing System will have several kinds of interactive interfaces capturing moving images, pictures and diagrams, voice and text. The internal structure of the machine will generalise on the knowledge based systems architecture shown in Chapter 5 and its networking capability will enable access to dedicated machines to carry out particular processing tasks.

Figure 8.3 produced by researcher Kinji Takei at the conference shows ICOT's estimation of the relationship between the domains of application of conventional and Fifth Generation computing.

A shift in the method of system design to accommodate the changing nature of application development was hinted at in various ways throughout the Cambridge conference. Erik Sandewall speculated on a move towards "executable application modules" (Figure 7.7). Richard Ennals noted the switch from procedural to declarative programming.

Daniel Sagalowicz offered a conservative view of the implications for system developers in his speculation on the range of skills which might be required for the adoption of AI techniques. This may be contrasted with Richard Ennals' comments in section 2.10 above. Sagalowicz started with the *end user*, who, in his opinion, should not require any special training if the end product is a complete system with comprehensive knowledge.

The person who will *maintain* an existing expert system will require training. After the system is there, its software tool has been chosen, and the architecture for most of the knowledge base has been implemented, it will still require amendment as the field of expertise moves and changes. It may take maintenance staff two or three weeks to learn about the system, to learn what is in the knowledge base and to make the necessary minor improvements. Most contemporary computer programmers would be able to undertake this kind of job with minimal training.

A third type of person involved in the diffusion of these AI techniques will be the real high level *knowledge engineer*. He or she will go and interview the expert and decide which tool will be used to develop the knowledge system, and how the knowledge base will

Figure 8.2: Image of a fifth generation system

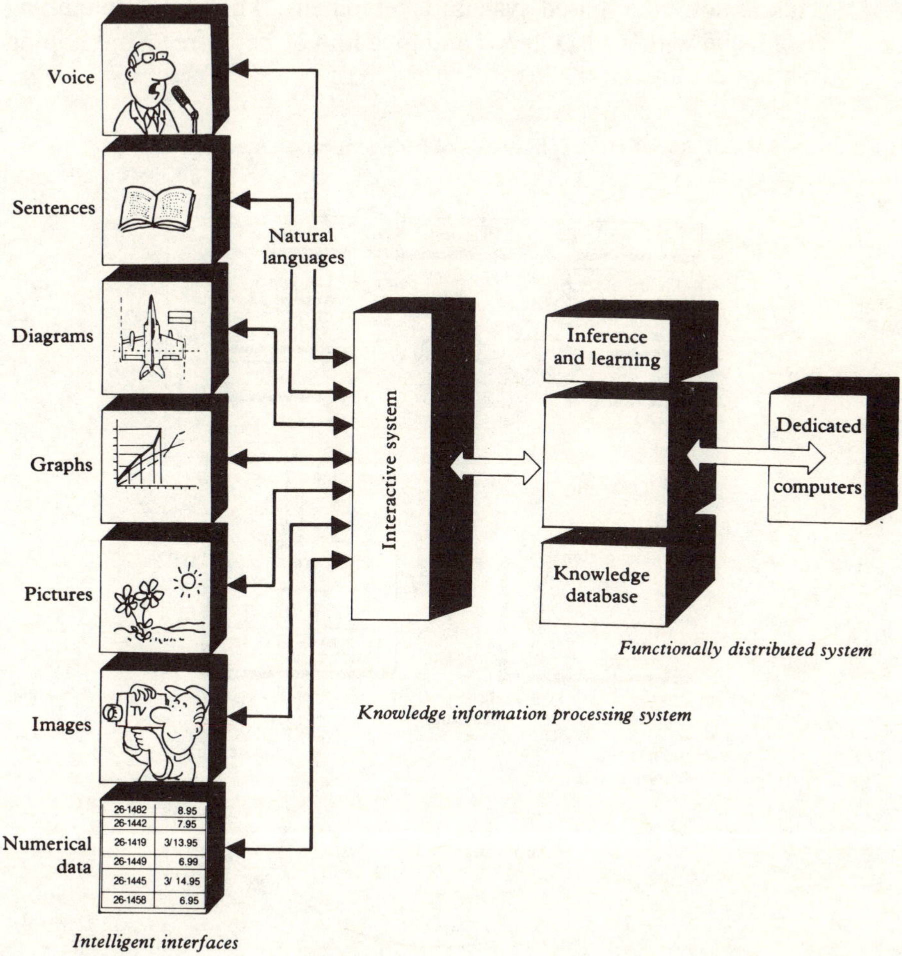

be organised. Such a person will need a lot of training and experience in creating knowledge systems. He should have participated in two or three system developments before being able to be in a position to design a new system with reasonable confidence.

Then there is a fourth category, the *creator* of the new tools. These are the people who are going to build the next EMYCIN, the next PROSPECTOR and the PROSPECTORs of years to come. They will need to have a lot of experience in custom systems and a lot of experience in AI. They must be up to date on AI research.

Since there are substantial lead times involved in the necessary learning and training, new responsibilities are placed on vendors and users.

According to Sagalowicz there are basically three ways to undertake knowledge based system development. The first is to employ someone with a PhD in AI, and give him or her a free hand hoping

Figure 8.3: Applications of fifth generation system

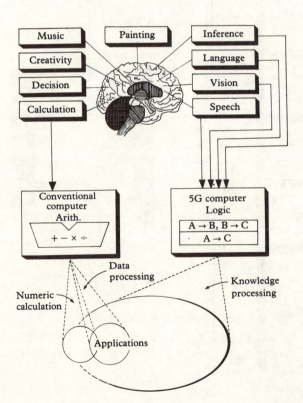

that in a few years something will have been produced. The second way is to take a group of computer professionals and give them an initial tool with some specific problems to solve. It will still probably take a year or two for these people to do enough throwaway systems and get sufficient experience so that at the end of that time they can do a reasonable job developing the next system for the company. The third way, which has been promoted typically by the vendors, is to buy-in vendors to construct a custom system which will demonstrate that a particular problem is soluble and in the course of its solution to train the company's own staff and thus transfer the technology.

The key role here is played by the vendors who are the main market makers. The market does not appear all of a sudden overnight. In the US the push comes from the vendor and in fact from the venture capitalist, this enables the market to be opened up. At the present time the US market leads Europe by two to three years in this respect.

In the future computer manufacturers will probably provide basic software tools. There will be room for specialised companies to provide slightly more advanced tools with respect to the computer manufacturers. Software houses will help customers design knowledge systems which correspond to their particular problem. And finally, the users themselves will have to build an organisation to produce bread and butter systems where they do not want this expertise to go outside their companies.

It is the latter group who may ultimately be the most significant. This is because the changes will be taking place within the context of a radical re-organisation of the division of office work – prompted by the switch from the typewriter and the telephone to the integrated information system. The old pattern of strict separation of management and operating functions, as shown in Figure 8.4, is already breaking down. Paul Strassmann of Xerox has speculated that a new pattern which re-integrates these two functions in new kinds of jobs is already emerging.

8.6   Implications for information systems research

Throughout the conference these broader organisational possibilities and problems were hinted at. Hermann Hauser of Acorn Computers argued that quite primitive tools made universally available could inspire virtuoso solutions. He described how one of Acorn's first products had incorporated a loudspeaker switched by a single register to produce a beep. A few months after the product had been launched, a 14-year-old boy sent the company a program that played a four voice fugue. The design of more sophisticated development environments than his, with enhanced capacity to support end user creativity, is an important area of research.

Erik Sandewall showed in his essay one way of exploiting the new methods of programming while using contemporary languages and machines, that both is effective in stimulating the creativity of users, and can ease the ultimate transition to new hardware and software. He argued that the development of 4th Generation software, and programs like VISICALC and outline processors, are already precursors of these new software development techniques.

Roger Needham spoke of the research questions which followed from the construction of wide-flung systems. Today the most widespread network is that of the telephone system which has some 600 million or more machines capable of interconnection. This network functions largely because telephones are rather passive and lacking in initiative. This is not the case with computers. As computers have become universal, they have acquired a strong tendency to communicate with each other in order to carry out their functions. This gives rise to several distinct problems of scale in large distributed systems.

Professor Needham called this "the 100,000 computer problem". He believed that there were two significant thresholds as the complexity of distributed systems grew. With a very small system, a "toy distributed system" perhaps, you could go to the person responsible for it, ask what each computer does, and be told the functions of each of the machines in the network. A first threshold is crossed when the person in charge of the system responds by saying "I don't actually know what there is in the system, but we could find out fairly easily". He might then direct you to an administrator who can produce a system design.

The next threshold comes when it is impossible for anyone at all to answer the question about what's in the system and what it is used for. This stage can be reached when there are some three or four thousand computers involved. It is very difficult to organise that scale of configuration in a way that won't fail in horrible ways as the numbers increase, either because somewhere in it is buried an algorithm which is worse than linear in its performance as the number of participants grows, or message communication goes up in a similarly disastrous fashion, or some other problem occurs.

There are several research issues here. One might be called the

Figure 8.4: Administrative organisation *(based on Strassmann 1985)*

(a) *Traditional administrative organisation*

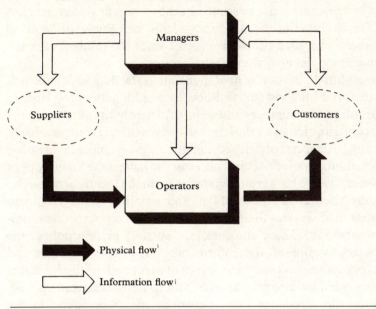

(b) *Future administrative organisation*

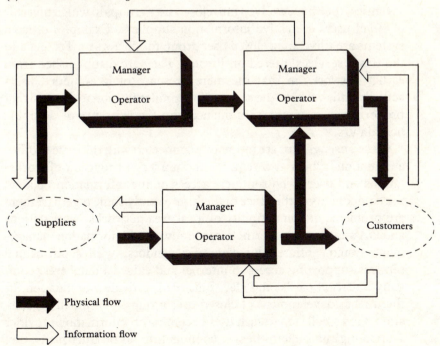

"non-up-to-dateness problem". In small systems it is possible to ensure that everyone has an up-to-date version of the system. In bigger systems this is not possible but the system must nevertheless continue to function at all times. It is extremely difficult to experiment with such problems of scale since the resources are not easy to come by in an academic environment.

The essential question is how to maintain the data which records the structure of the system, and how to avoid it getting too large in proportion to the numbers and kept sufficiently up to date for the whole configuration to work. It is well known that it is not possible to keep it up to date completely. Although this is a technical area rather than an administrative one, it is necessary to have some knowledge of the administrative background in order to do the technical research.

Finally, there are the range of issues surrounding the development of value added services to be offered over such computer communication networks. These are questions such as pricing policy, the proprietary nature of the information provided, protocols and regulatory issues, and software design matters such as the functions to be provided by directory servers, and conferencing systems, etc. Although the origins of these networks are to be found in the timesharing and bibliographic data services of the sixties and seventies, they have evolved into closed user groups in which myriads of small users are active information suppliers. Examples of such systems are Phycom, a closed user group for doctors on Telenet and the travel services offered on Prestel. They are distinguished from earlier networks in that the mere presence of like-minded users actually adds value to the service, in a similar fashion to the way that property values might be influenced by the existence of desirable neighbours.

Closed user groups are intimately connected with the issue of office automation, which also requires the universal provision of workstations and users who routinely access online information. Today, the components of the office of the future rarely come together; there are problems of compatibility of local area networks, workstations and OA strategies. Nevertheless, the advanced information management systems offered by computer vendors, with sophisticated services supporting access to internal and external databases, company bulletin boards, and electronic mail, provide a foundation for the further development of closed user groups. Within an organisation it is a small step to each user becoming an information provider – updating the bulletin board, commenting on product plans, etc.

The existence of such an internal online environment sets the stage for the emergence of industry specific closed user groups offering appropriate application software and peer communications.

8.7 Conclusions

In this essay we have looked at various approaches to the implementation of AI techniques within the context of large scale information systems. We have seen how a new range of development tools which run today on special purpose and expensive hardware, are being used to push forward the application of natural language and knowledge based systems. We can expect that falling hardware costs, and the interim achievements of the Japanese Fifth Generation Programme and its emulators will speed the take up of these techniques. However, the environment in which the new systems will run, both human and computer, will become increasingly complex as information systems proliferate, posing considerable challenges to system developers and researchers alike.

References and suggestions for further reading

AI Magazine and *AAAI Proceedings*. American Association for Artificial Intelligence, 445 Burgess Drive, Menlo Park, CA 94025, USA.

AI Marketing, AIM Publications, P O Box 156, Natick, MA 01760, USA.

AISB Quarterly, Society for the Study of Artificial Intelligence and the Simulation of Behaviour, Ben du Boulay, SSAISB Treasurer, Cognitive Studies Programme, Arts Building, University of Sussex, Brighton, BN1 9UN.

Artificial Intelligence Report, AI Publications, 95 First St, Los Altos, CA 94022, USA.

BCS Expert Systems Group, British Computer Society, 13 Mansfield Street, London, W1M OBP, UK.

Computational Linguistics. Association for Computational Linguistics. Donald E Walker, ACL Secretary-Treasurer, Bell Communications Research, 445 South Street, MRE 2A-379, Morristown, NJ 07960, USA.

Dahl, O.J., Nygaard, K. (1965). *SIMULA – A Language for Programming and Description of Discrete Event Systems*. NCC Publication No. 11, 1965. Oslo: Norwegian Computing Centre

Dahl, O-J, Myhrhaug, B., Nygaard, K. (1968). *SIMULA 67 Common Base Language*. NCC Publications S-2, 1968. Oslo: Norwegian Computing Centre.

ECCAI Quarterly. European Coordinating Committee for Artificial Intelligence. Wolfgang Bibel, Chairman, I.f.Informatik TUM, Postfach 202420, D-8000 Munich 2, West Germany.

Goldberg, A. & Robson, D. (1983). *Smalltalk-80*, The Language and its Implementation, London: Addison-Wesley.

International Directory of Artificial Intelligence Companies, Artificial Intelligence Software, P O Box 198, 45100 Rovigo, Italy.

Strassmann, Paul A. (1985) *Information Payoff*. London: Collier MacMillan. New York: Free Press.

Winston, P.H. and Prendergast, K.A. (eds.). (1984) The *AI Business*. Cambridge, Mass: MIT Press

9
RICHARD ENNALS
New research infrastructures

9.1   Introduction

Governments and commercial companies have more than an academic interest in the outcomes of research and development programmes in advanced information technology. They regard a strong capability in this area as essential for economic reasons. The Alvey Report in the United Kingdom put forward arguments for a national collaborative programme that were repeated in many other countries:

1. The world IT market is growing. The UK needs a large share, but is declining at present.
2. We need competitive levels of achievement in certain fundamental enabling technologies.
3. These enabling technologies are the necessary supporting infrastructures and can be identified now.
4. We require a strong domestic capability in these technologies.
5. A national collaborative effort is required. This means government backing.

The choices were summed up in clear terms:

> The issue before us is stark. We can either seek to be at the leading edge of these technologies; or we can aim to rely upon imported technology; or we opt out of the race.

A large proportion of the recommendations of that report were accepted. The challenge now, in each of the programmes of research and development around the world, is to construct a solution to the problem whose description has been accepted.

Different solutions in terms of new research infrastructures have emerged in different programmes, influenced by historical, economic and political circumstances, as well as by what are taken as appropriate models of experience elsewhere. One such model has clearly been SRI International, established for thirty years, and the base for the authors of many of the previous chapters. The degree of influence of technical researchers has varied, as has the experience and competence of those faced with responsibilities of research management. Whatever new research infrastructures are established, some of the same issues have to be faced.

In this chapter we will examine case studies of new infrastructures, identifying some of the common issues, and conclude with some suggestions as to how we may proceed from academic research to industrial applications that can be of general social and economic benefit.

At the Cambridge conference speakers dealing with this subject were presented with six questions to assist in structuring their presentations and the ensuing discussion. They were not always answered, but they were as follows:

1. What is new about your research institution?
2. Do we need long-term planning?
3. How can we cope with problems of manpower?
4. How can we take account of the social and economic implications of our work?
5. Can there be such a thing as precompetitive research in a competitive world?
6. What scope is there here for international cooperation?

9.2 The traditional relationship between academia and industry

Dr Geoffrey Robinson of the IBM UK Science Centre gave a cogent account at the conference of the relationship between academia and industry, without taking into account recent initiatives and changes. Motivating interests, he said, are different:

> In academia one is very interested in pursuing knowledge, one's work is entirely in the public domain, and one is interested in long-term research. In industry, traditionally,

we are very oriented by products. In IBM in particular, and in industry in general, there is an obsessive air of secrecy and confidentiality about what you are up to. Naturally, one tends to focus much more on short and mid-term goals than long-term ones.

In the real world, both sides suffer shortages. IBM sees it as possible for both sides to benefit from some kind of relationship:

In industry we find ourselves with some quite specific skill shortages, particularly in some scientific disciplines, in new application areas, and so on....In universities there is a shortage of money, there is a shortage of computer equipment and one can imagine that the reasons for academia and industry to get together and collaborate on research are much stronger in IT than perhaps in many other disciplines.

One should not expect collaboration to be easy, according to Robinson:

The driving forces of research in academia, the pressures from the academic environment, are on openness, on scientific truth, pursuit of knowledge, on peer reputation from one's peer researchers. In industry we have problems of confidentiality, timing, product leads, and so on, and the pressures on us tend to pull us apart rather than together. Then on top of all that we have the dreary logistic problems of organisation and of finance. Even geography can be a terrible problem if you are trying to collaborate with people.

There is in this last sentence an echo of Professor Needham's identification, at the same conference, of the weak link in present and past computer systems: people. Needham observed that:

A very important component of the system has not changed whatsoever, and shows no sign of doing so, and that's us. We are no better than we ever were at understanding complex systems that have got to work.

Systems here should be taken to include research programmes.

9.3   New research infrastructures in Japan

In one sense the Fifth Generation Project is nothing new for Japan. As outlined in the earlier chapter on national strategies, it is simply one in a series of national or government-funded projects which have covered wide areas of information and associated technologies. Long term planning is seen as inherent to high technology research and development.

As Professor Aiso stated in Cambridge, such a project is not based on the assumption of financial profit. The facilities of high quality government laboratories are available, together with a supply of well qualified researchers. The official view is that:

> the success of the project partly depends on whether or not there are well qualified people who are working for the project really hard.

Aiso acknowledged the importance of the tradition of cooperation:

> We have already established very good tripartite cooperation of university, industry and government. In particular, Japanese computer manufacturers have had long experience cooperating with each other on official projects. It is quite natural that when there is government funding cooperation between companies usually takes place in Japanese industry.

This tradition is reinforced by the high costs of fundamental research in this field, which make collaboration essential. The eight leading Japanese computer manufacturers have seconded staff to the ICOT research centre, while also retaining separate company research laboratories which undertake related work. Coordination is provided by staff from the government Electro-Technical Laboratory. The project is seen to be the responsibility of industry, and though university academics serve on advisory committees and engage in related projects in areas such as expert systems, there are no staff at ICOT seconded from academia.

We will return frequently to the question of manpower. Japan is unusual in that there is a tradition of extensive in-house or continuing education which is seen as an excellent substitute for a formal research education at university. Furthermore, the commitment to lifelong employment enhances the capacity of the individual and the company to take on long-term research projects. ICOT itself is regarded as making a major contribution to the advanced education of young researchers from industry.

There have been criticisms from Western observers that the structure and management style of the Fifth Generation Project has been rigid and hierarchical. A visitor to ICOT will notice that the structure of the Institute reflects the structure of the project as described in its published reports, with separate laboratories and research sub-groups working in parallel and communicating their results and requirements. The results of the initial stage suggest not only that the technical programme is on schedule, but that the commercial exploitation of the Mitsubishi PSI machine may be imminent, followed by applications systems and a high-specification low-cost super personal computer at the end of the decade.

ICOT has welcomed visiting scientists, and has sought to apply their ideas. It has developed links with foreign research groups, but has been less inclined to form alliances with foreign companies. Professor Aiso proposed a continuing programme of information exchange, international workshops and conferences, and scientific visits and exchanges.

David Brandin of SRI was chair of a US Department of Commerce panel on Japanese Technology, which concluded that much of the Japanese strength in advanced information technology derived not from a world lead in basic research, but from their unrivalled expertise in technology transfer. If other countries are to emulate their success in developing industrial applications, they will have to pay more attention to the appropriate mechanisms for technology transfer, and not focus merely on the technical research issues. It will not be enough to simply copy the "Japanese model", or for instance the "SRI model" of technology transfer, as circumstances vary greatly.

9.4   Research infrastructures in the Alvey and ESPRIT programmes

There is not a tradition in the United Kingdom or in Western Europe generally of collaboration between companies, between companies and government, between companies and universities, or between groups across national boundaries. In that sense therefore the infrastructures of the Alvey and ESPRIT programmes have a wider significance than merely that which is implied by the technical content of their programmes, important though that is. They constitute experiments in themselves, extending the frontiers of management and administrative science. All of the participants are to differing degrees feeling their way, and the sponsoring governments have expressed no long term commitment to what might be perceived as an interventionist approach in a key economic area.

In both programmes human resources are severely stretched. In the Alvey programme, for example, the Directorate has a focal role in policy and strategy generation and implementation, placing contracts and conducting relations with ESPRIT. The eight directors have been seconded from industry, the Department of Trade and Industry, the Ministry of Defence and the Science and Engineering Research Council. They can call on the services of various advisory bodies, but are limited to a maximum of 30 support staff.

The Alvey programme does not follow all of the recommendations of the Alvey Report. In particular, whereas the Report recommended that fundamental research projects should enjoy 90% government support, requiring industry to meet only 10% of their costs on long-term research, in the programme companies are obliged to contribute 50% of their costs, though the costs of academic participants are met in full. Furthermore, it is not now possible to engage in fundamental research in information technology without an industrial sponsor, or "uncle".

The Alvey directorate are playing a coordinating role, providing support in terms of hardware and communications, and seeking to form new research consortia and clubs in accordance with the overall objectives of the programme in enabling technology.

There are undoubted tensions, with varying perceptions as to the purpose of the programme. Some large companies see it as a programme of government aid to industry, under which they can have arrangements for contract research with universities on easier terms. University research groups such as those at Imperial College and Edinburgh University, whose work is regarded internationally as central to Fifth Generation computing, have had some difficulty in achieving recognition with companies who have not themselves undertaken research activities.

British expenditure on research and development, apart from in the military field, has declined significantly by comparison with her industrial competitors. The Lighthill Report of 1973 led to the cessation of most government funding for research in artificial intelligence, and companies have continued to disband research groups in recent years. Many leading firms either are unprepared to plan beyond the current products under development, or prefer to accumulate cash reserves, even buying back shares from shareholders.

Brian Oakley complained at the Cambridge conference about short term thinking in the British software industry, which has a good international reputation. He described problems in developing projects in software engineering:

> It is very difficult because the software industry is working flat out. It's growing very fast. The good people can all earn their keep all too easily and it's a very great temptation I believe for the firms not to make the investment in this field which they know that they should.

The same problem is experienced at ESPRIT with the same firms and their European counterparts. Penalties are also being paid for the change that obliges even small companies to meet 50% of their costs. Oakley observed:

> There is no doubt that it is difficult for a small firm to take a proper part in the Alvey programme at 50% funding. Frankly I think the real problem is whether a small company can spare the high quality manpower that is inevitably required for such work if the time horizon is reasonably long.

Although Oakley has stated the debt the Alvey programme owes to ICOT in administrative techniques, it is worth noting that the decision was made to set up no equivalent research centre in the United Kingdom. He argues that:

> There is always a danger in the West that if you set up a research centre it then does its own thing and nobody takes any notice because they haven't invented it.

At the same time an attempt is being made to build up centres of excellence where a critical mass of researchers in enabling technologies has been reached, and to develop means whereby the work of strategically important groups can be fed into a variety of collaborative projects. This is particularly true of Imperial College, and Edinburgh, Cambridge and Manchester Universities. Particularly in the IKBS area, the directorate are coordinating specialist national initiatives in an unprecedented manner.

The Alvey programme has to live with the consequences of previous research approaches and infrastructures, rather than following an established tradition as in Japan. This has surfaced particularly in the negotiation of collaboration agreements for research contracts. Few companies have experience of similar contracts (which in itself has led to the failure of many of their proposals to ESPRIT), and there is little case law on which to build. Critical difficulties remain in the areas predicted above by Geoffrey Robinson. His own company, IBM, is itself the cause of some controversy, having managed to secure funded participation in both the Alvey and ESPRIT programmes.

Pre-competitive collaboration underlies the concept of enabling technologies enshrined in the Alvey Report. It is not so evident in the detailed negotiation of collaboration agreements, many of which turn on the allocation of percentages of royalties to be paid on the sale of "deliverable" items during the progress of the project. Perhaps it is unsurprising in a project with an assured life of only five years, but there is little evidence of long term thinking among commercial participants. A notable exception would be the research consortium formed to develop the ALICE machine from Imperial College, a highly parallel computer that would appear to have a world lead, initially using the Inmos transputer, and providing a declarative programming environment for logic and functional programming. The consortium includes ICL, Plessey, Imperial College and Manchester University.

The Alvey directorate have sought international collaboration, not merely as the British representatives of ESPRIT, but between companies in Britain and Japan. ICL and Logica have also separately established contacts. The directorate remain sceptical about overseas industrial collaboration with British academics, leading to exploitation of their ideas by Britain's industrial competitors. Researchers from Edinburgh and Imperial College have been visiting scientists at ICOT, and their work has been incorporated into ICOT research results.

9.5 Industrial collaboration: the European Computer Industry Research Centre (ECRC)

The work of the Centre was presented at the Cambridge conference by its director, Dr Hervé Gallaire, involving the principal computer manufacturers from West Germany (Siemens), France (Bull) and the United Kingdom (ICL). Despite their size they were dwarfed in their home markets by IBM and other overseas companies, and had little experience of the European market outside their own home countries. The Centre exists to help gain an understanding of how each of the companies operate, and how they could develop into new markets.

The principal reason why the collaborating companies established this separate initiative, apart from participating in ESPRIT and their separate national programmes, was that programmes such as ESPRIT did not provide for collaborative research in a common research centre (on the model of ICOT). This seemed to diminish the practical degree of collaboration that was possible, despite the ESPRIT criterion that projects should foster collaboration between companies and countries in the EEC.

The Munich research centre is a meeting place for the companies where they discuss long term programmes on a regular basis. Collaboration is not seen as precluding competition, especially when one of the goals is to penetrate one another's market.

The centre has had no public funding, and is concerned with work which may bear fruit in five or ten years. It has 50 researchers, many of them seconded by their companies as a means of technology transfer and exchange. The research themes correspond to those of ESPRIT and Alvey, and some of the researchers may come from universities or public research bodies. Overall the centre should be seen as complementary to the other European programmes described, but also tailored to the needs of the company "shareholders" in the centre.

9.6   Industrial collaboration: the Microelectronics and Computer Technology Corporation (MCC)

The work of the MCC was described at the Cambridge conference by Palle Smidt, its Senior Vice President, Programs and Plans. He set MCC in the context of American expenditure of $90bn per annum on research and development, 50% government-funded and 50% industrially funded. Of government-funded research, two-thirds was devoted to defence, of which 90% was development and some 10% applied and basic research. Of the industrially funded research, only some 4% was basic research, while 96% was applied research and product development.

MCC was established as a totally private-sector initiative, dealing exclusively in long term research. It was established for the profit of its shareholders, initially ten and now eighteen in number, who seek to use it to improve their competitiveness. Smidt emphasised that:

> MCC could be the most efficient developer of excellent research results, but if the results can't fast be brought into the commercial environment there would be absolutely no justification for MCC.

Planning was clearly involved in the corporation; for cooperative ventures, for normal business environments and in planning for states and federal governments.

9.7   Problems of research infrastructures: just a matter of profit and loss?

As a purely profit-motivated corporation, MCC could take a straightforward approach to issues which seem more complex for those concerned with the other research infrastructures discussed above.

When faced with the question of manpower, Palle Smidt replied:

> We have a very simple issue from an industrial point of

view. We have certain requirements and we need certain profiles of experience, and certain profiles of performance, and if they are not available we would take whatever action is required to get them.

By contrast Brian Oakley, speaking as director of a programme coordinated by government, found the problem of manpower extremely worrying:

> I have to say that I do not think that we are providing at the moment the necessary manpower which we will need both to pursue, satisfactorily, programmes like ESPRIT and Alvey, and really, what is more important, to feed the IT industries as they expand. In my view if there is a race for the Fifth Generation it will go to the country which concerns itself most with the provision of high quality manpower.

When asked about the social and economic implications of the work of MCC, Palle Smidt said:

> You have to appreciate that, coming from the private sector, the social and economic implications outside our industry are really not that relevant. We have a very simple vision, and that goes both for MCC and our shareholders. If we cannot increase the wealth of our owners, we have no relevance as participants in the business.

The Master of Churchill College, Professor Sir Herman Bondi, expressed a worry about the implications of the information that could now be provided:

> What happens to the information that becomes available and accessible through the new technologies? You have to have customers for it who are prepared to pay the very real costs of absorbing information however palatably and nicely it is presented.

Dr Jeremy Bray MP was concerned with the support of intelligent decision-making:

> I would also expect us to give strong support to linked decision support systems in government, business, public authorities, education and to individuals, with a high degree of autonomy to the individual persons and agents in the system.

Finally, on considering the scope for international cooperation, Smidt took an equally straightforward approach:

> It would be necessary to understand in broad international cooperation, that if one gives something, what will he get in

return? If that's not clearly understood, I think the foundation for international cooperation may be less, especially if it is undertaken within the private sector. The political or common view may be somewhat different from that.

In his closing address to the Cambridge conference, David Brandin of SRI explored the case for cooperation between the various research programmes. He observed what they have in common:

They constitute a science race among a collection of handicapped contestants all suffering from the same disability. For example, they all suffer from limited resources. There is not enough money in every programme. There are not enough facilities. There is a duplication of effort in most programmes in most countries, there are overlaps and there are gaps as well. The most serious problem of all is a lack of qualified people. Everybody suffers from a lack of qualified people, and yet all the programmes have the same objectives.

Recognising the political reasons that would prevent cooperation between all the overlapping programmes, he suggested that the real need in each programme was "to get more people to develop the technology". "Technology transfer", he observed, "takes place primarily with people."

9.8   Advanced information technology as if people mattered

Max Bramer, in his review of the Japanese Fifth Generation Computer Project, notes the emphasis placed there on people:

People are regarded as the key national resource. The Japanese workforce is probably the most highly educated in the world; ninety-four per cent of children attend school to age eighteen, compared with twenty-two per cent in the UK, and thirty-seven and a half per cent subsequently enter higher education, as against twelve per cent in the UK. Whereas the funding of UK universities has been drastically cut in recent years, the declared long-term aim of the Japanese government is to provide university education for every child.

While education is regarded by government simply as an expense, rather than as an investment in the next generation of citizens, the chances of developing a new generation of technology, let alone of applying it intelligently, are limited. Knowledge based systems, above all previous technologies, should exploit the expertise of their users and lead them into further learning.

The spread of microcomputers has possibly compounded the

problems of education and training, in that it has encouraged the growth of the myth "Teach everyone how to program or make computers and this will generate people who can make better computers". Governments have seized on the attraction of the quick available solution, and have installed large numbers of microcomputers in schools, colleges, and training institutions. Igor Aleksander, Professor in the Management of Information Technology at Imperial College has examined the problem, and is critical of conventional approaches:

> Teaching people to make current computer structures and to program them when the research community is endeavouring to alter such structures out of recognition and to replace programming by more "natural" means of communication (speech, vision, natural language) seems sheer lunacy.

Instead Aleksander recommends a twofold educational focus. Firstly students should be given a heightened understanding of the potential of ideal machines so that they can press for technological improvements rather than feeling threatened by them. Secondly, the kind of managerial opportunities which are created by information technology should form the foundation of most new business studies as well as forming the basis of re-education for current businessmen.

Re-education is a major problem for computer scientists, programmers and users. The conventional assumptions which have governed computer design and use are being called into question and radically revised. A view of computing that is based on sequential programs for single-processor machines is not adequate to deal with declarative programming of parallel machines. Courses that provide an ill-structured and outdated view of the subject do little service to their students. Experience suggests that a well-educated student in another area of specialism may fare better in knowledge based computing than the product of such a course. As the Alvey Report notes, university departments of computer science in the United Kingdom find it necessary to provide remedial courses for freshman undergraduates who enter with an Advanced Level qualification in computing.

The research community in advanced computing is small, and in its early years has been drawn from a variety of backgrounds. Workers in artificial intelligence, for example, come from the fields of computer science, psychology, linguistics, philosophy, mathematics and logic.

Many of the ablest researchers had early training and professional experience in a different discipline, such as management science or engineering. In order to take an active part in conferences and international collaborations, researchers need a facility in at least one foreign language, even if their first language is English. The argument at researcher level is then strongly in favour of a broadly based education, with experience in formal reasoning; in short, the best of our cultural tradition over the centuries.

A similar account can be given of the educational needs of less academically advanced users of computers. As knowledge based systems develop further, the user will be more concerned with the correct description of his problem area than with the precise way in which the computer sets about finding a solution. In a declarative programming system, the user will provide a description, or specification, which the system will transform into an efficient program. Many of the traditional roles of the programmer are likely to disappear as the system becomes more intelligent. Programmers, like hand-loom weavers before them, are likely to be displaced by the advancing technology.

The experience of experienced industrial computer users working in advanced research centres on a "technology transfer" basis is similar. It is important to identify a focal problem area, and to develop progressively more effective ways of describing it.

The same knowledge based technology that is the object of the courses and research projects can be a uniquely powerful tool for education and training. Doubts may be expressed as to the efficacy of today's expert systems as replacements for human experts. Few patients would prefer to be treated by MYCIN instead of a doctor, and few mining companies would rely exclusively on the advice of PROSPECTOR. On the other hand many American medical schools are making use of MYCIN for teaching diagnostic skills, providing valuable practice and advice to students without necessitating the presence of a human patient or a busy consultant. Systems in PROLOG that represent pieces of legislation can provide information for the lawyer and his client, support for the legal draftsman or training for the student of legal reasoning or civil servant. Such systems are now available on low-cost microcomputers, and are accessible to students from secondary school age.

The same microcomputer technology is now appearing in schools, colleges and commercial companies. The same software is being used to develop expert systems for power stations, to provide intelligent interfaces to large software systems such as statistical models, and to develop classroom materials for the teaching of history and humanities in secondary schools. Experience in the variety of applications areas feeds back to the core research group at Imperial College, and advances in one project can benefit others.

The potential in the field of industrial training is becoming apparent. For some time courses presented to multinational companies have used materials developed in the school classroom. Now that the companies are using the same personal computer hardware, but lack the experienced manpower to direct its use in expert systems applications, they are beginning to turn to colleges of further education where joint courses can be developed to meet the education and training needs of both sides, in collaboration with university research groups.

A further pressure on manpower thus develops, for the same small group of researchers concerned with key enabling technologies is also charged with contributing to applications projects both directly and indirectly, and with a technology transfer role working alongside seconded industrial researchers. Furthermore, a university research group will be involved in undergraduate and postgraduate teaching, and with the development of distance learning materials. In such research infrastructures a great burden of necessity falls on few shoulders, and management systems have to be designed to maximise the effect of their work.

9.9   Conclusions

The issue is far broader than research groups and the manpower needs of particular companies. Fifth Generation computers are not yet with us, but already powerful expert systems technology is available on low-cost machines. The technology has already partially escaped the control of its erstwhile political and commercial masters. How is it to be used, and by whom? Information technology is not of itself political, but in its use it is a powerful political tool. Wealthy political parties have used computer facilities for sophisticated opinion polling and election mailings. Such facilities could be provided for all. Governments use computers to help minimise their social security expenditure. They could also be used to help claimants obtain their full entitlements.

In one sense the issue does not just concern our relationship with computers and expert systems. It concerns our relationships with experts, and the way we solve problems in society. In the field of expert systems we have learnt to ask our system to explain its reasoning and conduct an intelligible dialogue. We have all encountered human experts who have been reluctant to do either. If we receive clear explanations from a legal or medical expert system, how will this affect our relationship with a human lawyer or doctor? Will some major professions be obliged to change their methods of working, affecting the social and economic infrastructure?

Interactive problem-solving systems, of which we have some glimpses with small example programs, raise further questions. To be most effective there will be an exchange of questions and answers between the user and the system, using perhaps symmetry between the two as a design principle, with the system drawing on large databases and collections of rules. Are there some questions which we are not prepared to answer, or which we wish to prevent the system or user from being able to ask? Will we revise our views of Freedom of Information legislation if access to information really is in the hands of the ordinary citizen? Do we live in a democratic society if knowledge and consequent power are concentrated in the hands of a minority?

Computer scientists are not accustomed to dealing with issues of politics and philosophy, which have not normally formed part of their education or professional background. The new generation of computers is too powerful to be left in the hands of the computer scientists. The new research infrastructure, if it is to produce the industrial applications for the social and economic benefit of society, must progressively broaden informed access to the technology.

References and suggestions for further reading

Aleksander, I. (1984). Myths that are spoiling Britains's IT chances. *Guardian*, 12th September.

Alvey, J. (1982). *A Programme for Advanced Information Technology*. The Report of the Alvey Committee. London: HMSO.

Benson, I. & Lloyd J. (1983). *New Technology and Industrial Change*. London: Kogan Page. New York: Nichols.

Bernal, J.D. (1954). *Science in History*. London: C.A Watts.

Bramer, M. (1984). The Japanese Fifth Generation Computer Project. In *New Information Technology*, ed. A. Burns. Chichester: Ellis Horwood.

Ennals, J.R. (1985). The importance of PROLOG in the role of programming. In *Teaching Informatics*, ed. M. Griffiths, E.D. Tagg. Amsterdam: North-Holland.

Ennals, J.R., Cotterell, A. (1985). *Implications of Fifth Generation Computers for Further Education*. London: Department of Education and Science.

Hayes, J.E., Michie, D. (eds.) (1983). *Intelligent Systems: The Unprecedented Opportunity*. Chichester: Ellis Horwood.

Servan-Schreiber, J.-J. (1981). *The World Challenge*. London: Collins.

Toffler, A. (1980). *The Third Wave*. London: Pan.

INDEX

CuP